Scenes from a Silent World

Felicia Skene

Table of Contents

Scenes from a Silent World

Felicia Skene

Do the darkness and the terror plot against you?
We also plan.
Those who love you are more than those who hate you—
Trust God, O man.—*From the Koran.*

NOTE.

THESE Papers originally appeared in 'Blackwood's Magazine,' and are now reprinted with an Introduction, large additions, and a new chapter upon Capital Punishment.

INTRODUCTION.

THIS work is the result of a real experience within the unseen prison world. It contains no element of fiction from beginning to end: it tells, as clearly and accurately as may be, the true histories of some who have lived and suffered and died in that hidden region of remorse and pain. Where the actual words they have used have not been quite distinctly remembered, the substance of their meaning has been given as plainly as possible. Whether the deductions we have drawn from these cases are correct or not, the facts themselves speak with the voice of truth; and we claim for that voice that it has a right to be heard by all who desire to help and benefit their fellow–creatures. There are many such, happily, in these days; but it may be said that among the seething masses of the poor within our crowded cities, in the workhouses, and hospitals, there is misery and anguish enough to exhaust all philanthropic energies, without seeking an aliment for them in the storehouses of criminals.

It is in the hope that we may be able to create a different impression by our Scenes from the Silent World, that we have brought them forth from their well–regulated obscurity.

If in all the distress and grief we see around us, that which is the most exceptionally bitter and hopeless has the greatest right to our sympathy and assistance, we may well claim it for the mournful wreckage of human life which is cast up on the gloomy prison strand from the ocean of this world's boundless suffering. There are elements in the agony of life as it is meted out to the inmates of a prison which have no place in the sorrows, cruel as they often are, of the poor and helpless without its walls. First and direst of the evils that weigh like a curse on the prisoner's existence, is the brand of crime, stamped on his inmost soul, no less than on his outer life, and all the more torturing that it is self–created. Is there any misfortune or trial, however heavy, which a man may not bear with serene courage, when he can hold his head erect in self–respect before his fellow–men, and with clear conscience look up to the free heavens and trust that they may yet smile on him with the sunshine of the love of God? But the blackness of the shadow which hangs for ever over the convicted criminal is that of a despair which seems to him irremediable both here and hereafter. Never while his mortal life lasts can the dark stain of his iniquity be hidden any more from the open gaze of his fellow–creatures; and he dares not hope that it can ever be effaced before the eyes of the Eternal Justice, if his mind be capable of imaging a life beyond the grave. Shame and disgrace will follow him when he passes through the prison gates. "Jail–bird," "felon," "convict,"—these are the epithets he will read in every look that meets him, if even he does not hear them loudly hurled at him. No man will trust him; none will have any dealings with him; he will be shunned by all: no honest employment will come within his reach; he must starve, or sin again to win a morsel of bread. Would that any words of ours could adequately reveal the depth and extent of a prisoner's utter hopelessness! Despairing of life, despairing of death, which he believes can lead to no heaven of hope for him,—does the world contain a more helplessly forlorn and desolate being than the guilt–convicted criminal? Does his anguish lack yet one sting?—it is in the thought that his wretchedness is all self–caused. Once he too was innocent, and could look up with fearless eyes to the wide pure skies: his own hand has dealt the death–blow to his honour and peace and freedom, and severed with keen relentless stroke the ties that bound him to his fellow–creatures. He is friendless for evermore; he has killed also the love and respect of those most dear to him; he is no longer the object of their affection; he is their disgrace;—for their own sakes he must strive that they shall never look upon his face again. Is this man deserving of no pity, no help, no effort to lift him out of the black gulf of his despair and set him upon the delectable hills, from whence he may yet catch a glimpse of the mercy of God and the sympathy of man? Surely of all who writhe in pain upon this lower earth, he most sorely needs the touch of human beneficence! But does he obtain it? Does not the world in general go on its way amid fair sights and engrossing interests, without one thought of those who are lying pent up in the perpetual gloom and silence of the prison walls? Unless some startling crime or exciting trial calls public attention to the Silent World, its denizens are left to pine out their dreary lives unheeded and unaided. We do not for a moment wish to ignore or undervalue such agencies as do exist in the present day for the relief and benefit of convicts,—prisoners' aid societies, police court missions, and other institutions, admirable so far as they go,—but these all deal with the criminal only after he is discharged from durance, when many opposing influences stand in the way to mar their efficacy. They cannot touch the man condemned to death, or to the harder fate of penal servitude for life, or even to a lengthened sentence. We know of no attempt among these agencies to reach prisoners during their period of incarceration, excepting one solitary effort in the shape of pious letters which are sent to prisoners at Christmas–tide, in order that they may have some little share in the goodwill and brotherly love called forth by that season. It is a kindly plan; but the writers of these well–meant epistles are, to the convicts, but nameless strangers,—they have never known them, and never will. The letters can only appear to them in the same light as a printed tract, and serve mainly to while away a few hours of the great annual festival which the prisoners spend exactly like a Sunday, no alteration even in their ordinary uninviting food being allowed to them.

Further, these efforts, such as they are, emanate from what may be called a handful of people, in comparison with the large majority we earnestly desire to interest in the Silent World and its inhabitants. It may be asked, through what means could any active interest be shown to them by the general public, when they are hidden away from their very knowledge behind immovable bolts and bars? This is undoubtedly true at present, but it is for that very reason that we have been anxious to make known the histories contained in this volume; for we cannot doubt that if public opinion were once aroused to the claims of these criminals on the charity and help of their fellow—mortals, the subject would be brought, perforce, under the consideration of those in authority; and we might then reasonably hope that it would have the desired effect of making the prisons in our land, homes of reformation and improvement, no less than of punishment. There are many different ways by which we believe this end might be attained, but the most efficacious would be the appointment of a properly constituted band of visitors, who would make personal acquaintance with every individual prisoner, and study his case in all its bearings, past and future, with a view to his amelioration.

Such a suggestion will be met by the conviction on the part of most persons who have thought on the subject, that it would only tend to create hypocrites and impostors among those of our "jail—birds," who are so hopelessly vicious and degraded that they are completely impervious to all good influences. We do not deny that such exist in the shape of professional thieves and villains, whose chief pleasure when at liberty is in cruelty and ruffianism of all kinds; but if only a small percentage of the prisoners were radically or permanently benefited, would not such a result be well worth all the efforts that could be made? And even in the case of those apparently utterly hopeless—who can say whether, at some stage of their after career, the memory of wise and true words spoken to them within the prison cells might not come back on them, to bear fruit in a tardy repentance?

There are, of course, many weighty considerations as to the treatment of criminals and the management of our penal establishments on which it would be manifest presumption in us to offer an opinion; but we do desire most earnestly to combat the theory put forward by some writers, that the subject is one which ought to be tabooed in polite society—that no good can possibly be done by prison revelations—that details from the lives of convicts are "nauseous" and "gruesome" (we quote expressions we have seen used), and that the most hopeless and wretched of all God's creatures ought to be left in well—merited oblivion by their happier brethren of the human race.

We cannot believe that such narrow and selfish views will long hold a place in this generation, when the best and noblest of its children are fired with the enthusiasm of humanity; and we venture to hope that the days are not far distant, when practical sympathy and earnest effort will follow the words which echo week by week from so many churches in our land—"That it may please Thee to show Thy pity upon all prisoners and captives."

SCENES FROM A SILENT WORLD.

CHAPTER I. A STRANGE LIFE AND DEATH.

"A man that were to sleep your sleep, and a hangman to help him to bed, I think he would change places with his officer; for look you, sir, you know not which way you shall go."

IT is well known, of course, that there exists in most of our large cities, behind all their din and traffic and ceaseless energy of human existence, a silent world where life, as vivid and eager as that which teems in the busy streets, is pent up, for ever unheard and unseen. But the full significance of that fact, with its dire import on some of the most complex problems of our time, can only be rightly apprehended by those who are allowed to enter there as habitual visitors, and to hold unrestrained intercourse with its inmates. This is a privilege for which permission must be given by the highest authorities, and it is not always easily obtained. It was granted, however, to the present writer, and it has resulted in a ten years' most intimate acquaintance with the very peculiar population which is to be found in those criminal establishments. Persons who pay a mere visit of curiosity to a prison, and are conducted by an official along rows of immaculately clean cells, where orderly prisoners are at work in perfect silence, cannot have the smallest conception of the extraordinary revelations in human nature, and in possibilities of human destiny, which are made known to those who are allowed to penetrate into the unveiled realities of the strange life that writhes within the impervious prison walls. Hidden there are elements of the deepest tragedy: abnormal facts, which raise the most intricate questions in moral responsibility and other psychological problems; true histories, equalling the wildest romance that imagination could picture; while on the other hand the daily routine is constantly enlivened by incidents that are irresistibly comic. Volumes might be filled with illustrations from all the various phases of prison life, and we purpose in these pages to give a selection from such as seem to us most striking and suggestive; but we desire especially to bring forward those which, besides their strong human interest, have an important bearing on a question that has always roused much diversity of opinion—that of the *Lex talionis*.

The capital penalty enforced by the existing law of England on all who, under any circumstances short of self–defence, destroy the life of a fellow–creature, stands on a totally different footing from any other legal punishment, inasmuch as it is one of which no human being can gauge the meaning or the extent. Sentences which are to be carried out within the limits of this mortal life can be exactly proportioned to the crime, dealing with a man's visible existence only, and leaving wholly untouched his possible destiny in other unknown spheres; but once commit him to the great mystery of death, and the living spirit passes from the hangman's hands into conditions absolutely impenetrable to us, and with which, therefore, it may well be doubted if we have any right to tamper. The usual arguments in favour of capital punishment, which affirm that it is a deterrent from crime—necessary for the public safety, and the only penalty dreaded by the criminal classes—were all met in a rather remarkable manner by certain cases which occurred in the prison with which the writer is connected. Three men, at short intervals of time, were brought to that gaol charged with precisely the same crime—the murder of their wives; but the individuals were in character and antecedents, and in many other respects, so entirely dissimilar, that the deductions to be drawn from their histories are very different in their nature. The case of the first we shall record, illustrates very strikingly the difficulty of holding the scales of justice evenly in those momentous decisions, where the lives of persons more or less criminal hang in the balance,—as well as some other considerations which will be sufficiently obvious from a simple recital of the facts.

Ted Brown, whose real name is not given for necessary reasons, was an elderly man, and when his age came to be questioned, he himself declared that he was upwards of eighty—but he was generally believed to be in fact about sixty years old. His family, which had originally consisted of fourteen children, had been reduced by accidents and disease to three alone—a grown–up daughter, and a quite young boy and girl. We have had a good deal of information lately, in various ways, respecting the very low state of civilisation which obtains among the poorer classes in our large towns, but it is scarcely possible to realise a life so completely on a level with that of the beasts of the field—if not below it—as was the normal existence of Ted Brown and his family. The man himself was not only absolutely illiterate, but of so low an order of intelligence that he was very happily characterised by one of the prison officials as the missing link which Darwinism seeks to find between our race and the Ascidians. It may really be doubted, however, whether any respectable gorilla would have demeaned himself to Ted Brown's level.

At the time when the event took place which brought him under the grasp of the law, Ted inhabited a mansion of his own construction, on an open common in the vicinity of a large town. It consisted of two or three old blankets suspended over upright sticks, so as to form a species of tent, in which he burrowed with his wife and two younger children. The eldest daughter had long before abandoned this uninviting family home, to get her living in a manner far from conducive to even the lowest standard of morals. The income of the whole party was limited to such small sums as could at irregular intervals be obtained by the manufacture of wooden pegs for clothes-lines, which were sold by Mrs Brown in the streets of the town, to which she was daily sent by her husband for that purpose. Ted himself meantime reclined luxuriously on a heap of straw in his airy abode, smoking the short black pipe which was the one possession in the world that was truly dear to his soul. His wife was therefore eminently useful to him. She did all the work, and procured the means of subsistence for the entire family, toiling from morning till night, while the life which her husband was enabled to lead by her labour, might have been compared to that of a Turkish Pasha in reduced circumstances. The woman was a poor simple creature, harmless enough, but with the mildest possible conception of the difference between right and wrong. She had lived with Ted for more than thirty years, and been the mother of his fourteen children, but she had not always been his wife; that dignity had been conferred upon her at a much later period, in the interests of the higher morality, by a benevolent clergyman who had come across them in the course of their wanderings from place to place. The couple had lived more or less harmoniously together till a few years previously, when Ted had been laid aside for a time by an attack of rheumatic fever—a malady which, considering the nature of his abode, might have been expected to fasten permanently on the whole family. During his compulsory retirement from this cause in some pauper hospital, he believed that his wife had acted in a manner to arouse his jealousy. For this offence, real or supposed, he never forgave her; and when any circumstance recalled it to his memory, he was in the habit of beating her in a very violent manner.

On a certain cold winter's night the family went to bed as usual—that is, they lay down on the ground of the open common, sheltered only by their blanket tent—the two children sleeping one on each side of their mother. Ted had bestowed high-sounding appellations on his progeny, which contrasted very oddly with their circumstances. The boy was invested with the titles as well as the name of a royal personage; and the girl was

7

endowed with a designation, probably taken from that of a ship, which was equivalent to the word Britannia. It was from her account that the events of that fatal night became known. She was apparently about ten or eleven years of age, though said to be older, and in her the resemblance to the gorilla tribe was quite as strongly marked as in her father. In all her ways and movements she was exactly like a monkey, with the one exception that she could speak with a human tongue, in the lowest dialect of her native county. According to her statement, she awoke on the night in question to find that her "dad"—stung probably by some sudden recollection of his grievance against his wife—was stretching across her in order to reach her "mammy," whom he was "hitting," as she expressed it, with great fierceness. Britannia lay still and watched the proceedings,—it was only what she had witnessed many times before; but on that starlit night Ted went further than he intended or knew. When at last he desisted, and turned round to go to sleep again, his unfortunate wife, who is not said to have uttered a single cry or complaint, "**scrawled**," to use Britannia's peculiar phraseology, out of the tent, apparently with the intention of getting some water to drink from a little streamlet which ran through the common at a few yards' distance. She did not return, and presently the child went out to see what had become of her. She found the poor woman lying quite dead, with her feet in the water. Britannia ran back to her father and told him that her mother would not move or speak. Ted rose and followed her to the spot she pointed out. There, in the dim starlight, he looked down into the dead woman's face, and gradually became aware of the result of the discipline to which he had subjected her. Having satisfied himself that life was extinct, he dragged her inanimate form back into the tent with the help of his little daughter. Then the remaining members of the family composedly lay down by the side of the corpse and slept till morning. So soon as the daylight dawned, Ted went out to gather sticks wherewith to kindle his fire, and being apparently somewhat embarrassed by the lifeless burden of which he had become possessed, he told Britannia to go to the cottage of a labouring man who had occasionally passed through the common and spoken a few friendly words to him, and tell him that he wished to see him.

This neighbour presently arrived, and Ted went cheerfully to meet him, carrying the sticks with which he was about to prepare his breakfast. He at once announced the tragic event of the preceding night in the following terms: "We have got a dead 'un here this morning." The labourer went into the tent, and what he saw there decided him to go for the nearest policeman, without any intimation of his intention to the family. That functionary speedily arrived, and had no doubt whatever as to his duty. On the following night Ted slept within four stone walls, sheltered from the wind and weather, the first time for many a year.

In due course he was brought to trial. His own little girl was the principal witness against him, and the judge, having heard Britannia's account of the tragedy, practically directed the jury to find him guilty of the wilful murder of his wife.

Now, as a matter of fact, Ted had been guilty of wilful cruelty to an extent which no doubt deserved severe punishment; but of wilful murder he was not either legally or morally guilty. To kill his wife was the very last thing he either wished or intended: not that he had any real love for her,—his pipe being, as we have said, the sole object of his affections,—but because the loss of her useful services would have rendered her death, even from natural causes, a most dis– astrous calamity to him. However, the usual grim sentence followed the verdict; and Ted—such as we have described him in his mental and moral characteristics—was left to face, within little more than a fortnight, what Carlyle was wont to call "the eternities."

The duty of preparing him for this tremendous change necessarily devolved on the prison chaplain, and all that zeal and earnestness could effect, that good man would undoubtedly have brought to bear on the task; but he was met at the very outset by a serious difficulty. Ted, in his cogitations over his terrible position, which was quite inexplicable to himself, had evolved out of his gorilla–like consciousness a very peculiar explanation of the whole affair. He became convinced that his impending doom, instead of being appointed by the law, was really a commercial transaction harmoniously arranged, for their own pecuniary benefit, between Jack Ketch and the chapel–man, by which names he designated the executioner and the clergyman. He imagined that they would be given an equivalent in money for value received, so soon as they could deliver up the strangled body of Ted Brown to the authorities; and as his life was decidedly precious to himself, he fixed in his own mind what he considered to be the very high sum of £5, as being the price bargained for by the two partners in the arrangement. When the chaplain, therefore, proceeded to the condemned cell to commence the course of theological training which was to fit Ted in seventeen days for an entrance on the eternal mysteries, he was dismayed by the very unexpected greeting with which he was received. Poor Ted fell prone upon his knees before him, and holding up beseeching hands, implored of him generously to forego the £2, 10s., which would be the clerical gentleman's share of the price to be paid for himself, when he should have been effectually done to death by the hangman's rope. If the chapel-man would thus give up his half of the gratuity, Ted considered it would be of no use for Jack Ketch to try and hold on to his fifty shillings, and he would be ready to make any amount of wooden pegs for them both in the course of his future career, so as to liquidate the debt which he would thus incur towards them. The unfortunate chapel-man was left to grapple with the difficulty of raising Ted, in one fortnight, from this level of intelligence respecting his position, to a fitting state of preparation for his departure into the realms unseen.

Meantime another person connected with the prison was occupied with the fate of the little Britannia.

It had been this child's evidence, and hers alone, which had brought her father to the scaffold; and as it had not been by any means to Ted's mind that the girl who had been his small slave all the days of her life should give a detailed account of his manners and customs in open court, he had glared upon her from the dock with a look of fury which she could not easily forget. In spite of her great affinity in many respects to the monkey tribe, Britannia had one prominent human trait, in her strong power of affection. The manner in which she attached herself with an absolutely blind trust to the prison visitor who took an interest in her was very touching; and it was evident, from her references to the scene at the trial, that in after years, if her intelligence were developed by education, the recollection of her own share in her father's fate, and his consequent rage against her, might be to her a source of lasting pain. Her friend was anxious, therefore, to win his forgiveness for her before the end, and arranged to have an interview with him for that purpose within a few hours of his execution. It seemed that the near approach of death was rousing some feelings of natural affection in Ted's darkened mind, and that it might afford him a gleam of comfort in his sad position, to hear that the child had been placed in a home where she would be kindly treated and provided for. To procure him this consolation, therefore, the arrangements for sending her to an orphanage a long distance from the city where he was waiting his doom were hastily concluded, and her friend went to visit her there, in order to receive from her some kind messages to be conveyed to the rapidly dying man. These plans were, however, instantly overthrown by that which is the bane of many of our modern schemes of benevolence—a species of moral red-tapism that surrounds otherwise useful charities with a number of petty stringent rules, so despotically maintained as often to frustrate entirely the good objects for which the institutions were founded. Instead of being able to receive Britannia's last messages to her father, the visitor was ushered into a committee-room, where a formidable circle of portentous–looking females announced that the poor half–monkey child had infringed certain small regulations of the establishment, and must be instantly dismissed, to find another home as best she could. The head and front of her offending appeared to be, that she had, with other reckless statements, informed a small companion that her father was about to be hanged, which information she had been ordered not to impart to any one.

Of course, if she were to be thus summarily expelled, all hope seemed at an end that the poor father, on the brink of death, could have the comfort of hearing she was safe in a permanent home, and this plea for her being retained was anxiously pressed on the redoubtable committee. The painful facts were heard with sphinx–like imperturbability, and the decision was repeated. The ladies wished the child to be removed, and the money which had been paid for a year's maintenance would be returned, deducting her board for the few days she had inhabited the house.

Fortunately a person of more liberal mind than this "charitable" committee, volunteered to give the poor child a home under the sad circumstances, and thus afford the unhappy man a last consolation. Having seen her safely housed under the kind care thus secured to her, Britannia's friend was therefore allowed to go to the condemned cell very shortly before the execution, to tell Ted that the child was definitely provided for, and to beg him to send her some kindly message of forgiveness, which would be a comfort to her in after years. The iron–banded door having been unlocked, the warder in charge was told to wait outside by a superior official, and a chair placed for the visitor, who took the dying criminal's band and said a few words to satisfy him, in the first instance, that it was a friend and not an enemy who had come to him; for poor Ted might well have arrived at the conclusion that all the persons who approached him were united in a conspiracy to remove him, as speedily as possible, from this visible sphere. Despite his affinity to the gorilla nature, Ted Brown was not insensible to the touch of human sympathy; and he never relaxed his grasp of the visitor's hand during the whole interview. It was somewhat like a bad dream to sit beside that strong, stalwart man, full of life and energy, and to know that in a few hours he would be lying stiff and stark under six feet of earth in the prison yard—and his own remarks, which reverted perpetually in a very curious manner to the fate awaiting him, did not tend to lessen this impression. Naturally he was anxious to explain his reasons for the peculiar treatment of his wife, which had terminated—to him so unexpectedly—in her death, and in touching on this topic he suddenly displayed a degree of delicacy which seemed strangely at variance with his grosser characteristics—he stopped short in his recital of her misdeeds, and asked leave to whisper to the officer present, some details which he did not consider fit for the ears of his visitor. It was, however, worse than useless that he should continue to go back over the irrevocable past; his future, of which the minutes might easily have been counted, was all that was left to him.

When the conversation was forcibly brought round to the subject of Britannia, he indulged at first in a fierce burst of passion against her for having brought him to the gallows; but he soon saw that this was very distasteful to his visitor, and poor Ted evidently thought that, in his critical position, it would be his wisest policy to try and please every one all round—so he changed his tone, and meekly agreed to do whatever was required of him with regard to the child.

"Yes, I'll forgive her," he said. "I'll not think no more of them lies she told, for all I never did nothink worse to my wife nor she deserved—a hussy! Just you think of it—me lying crippled up with the rheumatics, and her agoing flaunting out with that there fellow—"

"But about Britannia," interrupted the visitor, stopping these reminiscences—"you will send your love to her, will you not?"

"Yes, yes; you can tell her I bears no malice, and as how I hopes she'll grow up a bright woman;" and then he suddenly interpolated his paternal good wishes with the ghastly question—"Do you think, now, it will take them five minutes to kill me?"

The visitor was not experienced in details of the hanging process, but answered as soothingly as possible, and after a little time led him gently back to his child's message of love to him. This was at last quite effectual in reconciling him to her, and he even volunteered to "make up a letter," as he expressed it, to be given to her on the day of his death. Ted could neither read nor write, so this could only be done by dictation to one of the warders who watched him night and day, to prevent him from forestalling the hangman's work by any private proceedings of his own; but as it was likely to be a valuable document to the poor girl in the future, the offer was gladly accepted. A most extraordinary letter it proved to be: he had evidently thought it desirable to make it highly ecclesiastical, so that it consisted of the most curiously metamorphosed fragments from the chapel–man's teaching, interspersed with amazing reflections of Ted's own, and scraps of hymns heard in the Sunday services, inverted in such a manner as to become the most ineffable nonsense. The whole sum of Ted's religious knowledge when he first entered the prison had consisted in the following four lines, which he had quoted triumphantly as containing the entire body of sound doctrine taught by the Christian Church:—

"There are four corners to my bed,
And four angels at my head—
Matthew, Mark, Luke, and John,
Bless the bed that I lie on." After a fortnight's instruction, however, he had got hold of the idea of a lost sheep, and he put that unfortunate quadruped through its paces in his letter in a truly remarkable manner. Nevertheless, poor little Britannia, who is at this date gradually being educated into the semblance of a human being, will one day value very highly that strange message from the dead.

The end of the tragedy for poor gorilla—like Ted came in the shape of a fainting—fit, complete enough to produce total insensibility, into which he fell on the scaffold, from sheer terror of the death that overtook him before he recovered—and so terminates the history of the application of human justice to his individual case.

It is one of the peculiarities of the Silent World—where men and women have sometimes to expiate their offences by a dreadful death at the hands of their fellow—creatures—that the other criminals located there remain in total ignorance of the tragedy being enacted in their midst. The officers are never allowed to hold any communication with the convicts except such as may be necessary for the enforcement of discipline; and even the appointed visitor who is privileged to talk to them freely of their own concerns, is bound to adhere to the same rule with regard to all other subjects. Thus it is that the only prisoners who can have even a suspicion that an execution is going to take place under the very roof which shelters themselves, are the men who are told off to dig the grave of their yet living companion, on the day before his death.

It chanced, therefore, that the visitor had, during this same period, to pass from the ghastly associations of the condemned cell to the female prison, where the officials were being kept in a state of lively excitement by the proceedings of one of the inmates. While strange aspects of human nature and most pathetic histories are brought to light in intercourse with convicted women, it often happens that strangely eccentric characters appear among them, whose fantastic careers cannot be accounted for on any known principles of human action. Such an individual was No. 26, who was undergoing a long sentence in the same prison with Ted Brown at the time of his compulsory exit from it.

She was a tall, handsome woman, with fine features and brilliant black eyes, which were for ever flashing restlessly from side to side. She had been well educated, and carried herself with the air of a princess—maintaining in her quiet days a haughty demeanour, which she seldom relaxed, except in the case of the prison visitor, of whom she was graciously pleased to approve.

No. 26 shared in one invariable characteristic of female prisoners whose crimes have not been of the gravest type, that she was, according to her own account, a model of all the virtues. Women who are committed on charges of murder, manslaughter, or attempted suicide, are generally in too despairing a frame of mind to attempt any denial of the truth; but where their offences have been theft, assault, or other minor misdeeds, they systematically invent the most plausible explanations of the misadventure which has consigned them, as they affirm, in perfect innocence, to the prison cells. Sometimes, according to their statement, it has simply been the dense stupidity of the benighted judge who sentenced them, which has led to the catastrophe; but more frequently it has been a false friend, who has taken advantage of their confiding docility to shelter all manner of crimes behind their own immaculate virtue. The perpetual appearance of this stereotyped false friend, soon taught the visitor to dismiss the phantom on all occasions very summarily; and the imaginary deceiver of No. 26 having been so dealt with, she ceased any attempt to set aside the grim evidence given by the judicial record of her former convictions, and was fain to admit that she had been incarcerated many times before, for offences of various kinds. It soon became known that in every one of these prisons she had made the lives of the officials a burden to them, and some of her freaks were certainly of a very exasperating nature. On one occasion, when she was inhabiting the convict establishment of a large city, she announced that she had a complaint to make respecting the prison authorities, and demanded to be taken before the magistrates for that purpose. This is a request which is never denied to a prisoner who desires to bring forward any serious charge against the governing officials—and as No. 26 preserved an imperturbable silence on the subject of her grievance, it was concluded that it must be of a formidable nature. There was, therefore, quite an array of magistrates assembled to hear her statement, and the governor, chaplain, and other superior officers of the prison were summoned to be present. No. 26 was conducted before them, and solemnly ordered to proffer her accusation against those to whose custody she had been committed. She at once replied, in stately measured tones, that she felt it her duty to bring a charge against the chaplain,—the reverend gentleman there present,—for the criminal dulness of the wretched sermons to which he condemned his ill-used congregation Sunday after

Scenes from a Silent World

Sunday. They were not only quite worthless, she said, in style and composition, but also extremely illogical, inasmuch as he was perpetually attacking the female prisoners for their slight misdemeanours, while he passed lightly over the offences committed by the persons of his own sex on the male side of the prison. She requested that the magistrates would order an inquiry into his preaching powers, when she believed it would be found that he was possessed of none whatever. The countenance of the chaplain was seen to assume various shades of blue and green during this address, delivered much after the fashion of a counsel for the prosecution, until the magistrates could sufficiently overcome their smothered laughter to reprove the critical prisoner with befitting sternness, and order her immediate removal to her cell. A considerable time elapsed before she completed the term of her sentence in that city, and after a very brief period of liberty some fresh misdeeds consigned her to the jail which was the last home of Ted Brown.

When No. 26 came under the visitor's notice in her new compulsory retirement, she manifested so strong a desire to listen to advice and reform her ways on all points, that it was resolved to make a great effort to effect a radical change in her mode of disposing of her existence. It was known that her relations were highly respectable people, who had done their utmost for her many times, only to see her fall back into her wild lawless life more recklessly than before, and they had finally given her up in despair, and refused to recognise her at all. Plans were made, however, by the visitor for placing her in a position where she could begin a new life, and gain her own livelihood in an honest and suitable manner. She professed herself much pleased with the arrangement, which she knew involved considerable outlay, and the demons of passion and unrest with which she had been formerly possessed appeared to be completely laid. She went on thoroughly well till within a short time of the day when she was to obtain her discharge from prison, and then there was a lamentable change: she had scented the breath of freedom approaching speedily, and became simply intoxicated with it. One morning the visitor was met, on arriving at the jail, with the information that No. 26 had "broken out"—the prison term for a wild fit of seeming madness which from time to time seizes on the women confined within its walls. What had been the cause of this sudden attack?—there was literally no cause. The regulation breakfast had been brought as usual to No. 26, being absolutely identical with that provided for all the other women, when she had instantly burst into a wild fit of fury, declaring that her bread was less in weight than that destined for her companions. She tore off her cap, always an object of abhorrence, sent her long black hair flying out on the wind, and dashed like a maniac into the courtyard which separated her from the men's side of the prison, wrenching herself out of the hands of the officers who tried to control her. There she announced her intention of scaling the wall,—a feat that at any other time would have been absolutely impossible, but did not at that moment seem beyond the preternatural strength with which her passion had endowed her; and once on the other side, she declared she would make her way to the kitchen, take violent possession of the cook, a stout man some six feet high, and then and there boil him to a pulp in his own copper. These—the visitor was told—were her precise words, shouted out at the top of her voice; and although it had been found possible to prevent her from carrying out this unusual culinary operation, she could not be hindered from spreading ruin and devastation round her in the punishment- cell, to which she had been conveyed by the united efforts of a considerable number of prison officials. She had not been many minutes securely locked in there, when ominous sounds of a very violent description were heard to proceed from her abode; and a view of her position being taken through the inspection grating, she was seen standing clothed in dilapidated garments, and surrounded not only with everything the place contained smashed to atoms, but with quantities of the plaster and lime from the walls. She must have sprung at them like a wild cat to a considerable height, and she had succeeded in laying the actual stones bare to a very great extent. Enveloped in the clouds of dust she had raised, No. 26 poured forth such a volley of threats and blasphemous invectives against the officer, whose presence she detected behind the grating, that the visitor was strongly recommended not to attempt to have an interview with her—it was thought to be decidedly unsafe. That, however, was not the opinion of the individual in question, whose experience had shown that even the most lawless spirits can be tamed by kindness when once their affections have been roused. The idea of leaving the unfortunate No. 26 in the deplorable condition to which she had reduced herself was not to be entertained for a moment. By dint of obstinate insistence on the right of seeing any prisoner in that portion of the jail, however refractory, the visitor had the door of the punishment–cell opened, and entered it alone, knowing well that the presence of an official would have been fatal to any hope of quieting the woman. Certainly there proved to be no need for the least exercise of courage. The moment No. 26 saw her friend, she stopped short in a renewed attack she was making on the walls, let her hands fall by her sides, and opened wide her great black eyes in a look first of amazement, then of distress.

"You!" she exclaimed at last,—"is it really you come into this horrible place! I could not have dreamt that you would come here! If I had only known it, I would never have made such a frightful mess—I never thought for a moment you would have to stand in the midst of it! Stay; you must not set your feet in all that rubbish,"—and quickly tearing off a handkerchief which covered her shoulders, she went down on her knees and spread it on the stone floor of the cell—insisting that the visitor's feet should be placed on it, so that they might avoid all contact with the heaps of lime and dust she had accumulated there. It was a touching instance of the good feeling which underlay poor No. 26's fiendish temper, and which generally does exist more or less, even in the most brutalised prisoners.

A quiet conversation followed, during which she became perfectly meek, and really remorseful for her conduct. Unfortunately she could not always be under influences of this description—prison rules required the infliction of penalties for her insubordination, and poor No. 26 soon forgot her temporary conversion and went from bad to worse, till the day of her discharge arrived. By that time she had succeeded in inventing serious charges against every one of the prison authorities, from the governor downwards, including even the once–favoured visitor; and she announced her in– tention of making their various iniquities fully known to the world, by proclaiming them aloud, during her very first moments of freedom, when she would walk for that purpose through the public streets of the city in which the prison was situated.

As it was decidedly desirable to prevent such a proceeding, if possible, No. 26 was told that her railway fare would be paid to a place at a distance, where it was known she really wished to go, and an elderly warder was desired to accompany her to the station and see her safe off. He did not relish his task, but scarcely anticipated the extent of his difficulties. The moment No. 26 found herself outside the door of the prison, she knew that she was a perfectly free woman, and that the authorities had no longer any power over her, whereupon she gave the reins to her capricious temper, and declared that she would not go to the station till she had carried out her purpose of marching through the streets of the town, and there publicly announcing that the once respected officials of the jail were arrant villains, one and all.

At that moment the chaplain, most unfortunately for himself, came in at the outer gate, and instantly darting towards him, No. 26 collared him, metaphorically, and violently demanded instant redress for her injuries, while the officers still remaining safely within the walls looked out from the windows, and, it is to be feared, greatly enjoyed the scene. The elderly warder was, however, equal to the occasion. He blandly approached the woman while she was executing a species of fancy dance round the passive form of the dismayed clergyman, and reminded her that if she carried out her plan of a public denunciation of the prison authorities in the open streets, she would thereby reveal the disagreeable fact that she had herself been a denizen of that unsatisfactory abode; whereas, if she accompanied him to the station with all the airs and graces she could so well assume, it would be concluded that she was simply a fascinating lady, being escorted by an admiring gentleman on a journey of pleasure.

These tactics prevailed. No. 26 released the chaplain, whom she, like the Ancient Mariner, had been holding with her glittering eye, and departed elegantly for the station. Thither she arrived, after having had one or two renewed outbursts on the way, which the warder afterwards declared had sent a cold tremor through him; but he at last succeeded in getting her into the train, and returned home in an exhausted condition.

It might seem at first sight as if this system of periodical "breakings out," which is largely adopted by the lower class of female prisoners, were a mere unreasoning indulgence in temper; but it is not so—it has a distinct **rationale** of its own, illogical enough, no doubt, but a well−considered method in the apparent madness. The object of it is simply one of deliberate revenge for the pains and penalties to which their imprisonment subjects them. The women are perfectly aware that by these paroxysms of violence they give a great deal of trouble and annoyance to the officers, whose duty it is to carry out all the unpleasant conditions of the sentences they have brought on themselves by their offences against the law. And it is really extraordinary what an amount of extra punishment they will willingly undergo in order to have the gratification of thus revenging themselves. We had a curious instance of this on one occasion. A woman who had frequently been imprisoned for small offences was brought before the magistrates, on a charge which would only have involved the detention of a few weeks. She prided herself on her elegance of manner and diction, having in former times been a governess; and nothing could be more meek or graceful than the way in which she pleaded with the magistrates to let her off for once. She assured them that if they abstained from sending her to prison, she would immediately retire into a virtuous seclusion, and enter on a course of the highest morality. They were deaf to her entreaties, however, and felt bound to inflict on her what was really a very lenient sentence. No sooner was it pronounced, and the police were approaching to remove her, than she executed with amazing dexterity the plan which had been in her mind from the first. During the very time when she was mildly pleading for indulgence, she had managed, by a subtle unseen movement, to remove one of her shoes, and hide it under her shawl: and the moment the chief magistrate ceased speaking she drew it out, as quick as lightning, from its concealment, and flung it at his head with such precision of aim as effectually to land it in the position she most desired. Of course the result of such an outrage on the judicial dignity was the immediate doubling of her sentence under severe conditions. But that was simply nothing to her, in comparison with the exquisite enjoyment of that moment, when she saw her muddy old shoe flying through the air to lodge on the magisterial cranium. Even when she spoke of it afterwards in the presence of the visitor, to whom she wished to be abnormally respectful, she had difficulty in repressing her shrieks of delight at the recollection of that ineffable moment.

These are merely the lighter aspects of prison life; but they can only afford a very passing relief to the sadness and pain which must habitually weigh on those who are brought in contact with all the dark and tragic episodes that usually mark the records of that strange silent world.

Our connection with it has mainly brought before us the more serious conditions of convict existence; and we venture to hope that what has been learned by practical experience as the appointed visitor of a model jail, may prove usefully suggestive to some of those who are concerned in the administration of the law and the general treatment of criminals.

CHAPTER II. THE END OF A BITTER EXPERIENCE.

"With anguish of travail, until night
Shall they steer into shipwreck out of sight:
And with oars that break, and shrouds that strain,
Shall they drive whence no ship steers again."**THE** history of the last fifty years seems to indicate that it is the mission of the nineteenth century, at least in this country, to make a searching examination into the condition of most of our time–honoured institutions, whether social, moral, or religious, and expose, without mercy, any error or weakness in their *modus operandi*. It is to be hoped, therefore, that this active spirit of investigation may now be turned more seriously than has hitherto been the case, to the various branches of our existing criminal law, and especi– ally to that which ordains the infliction of a punishment that is irrevocable.

Scenes from a Silent World

In spite of the well–known fact that there has always been an influential minority in England who doubt the expediency of the capital penalty, and that the question has been repeatedly raised in Parliament, only to be summarily dismissed with the stock arguments on the subject,—the prejudice in its favour continues to be so strong amongst us, that we have not even arrived at any consideration of a desirable change in the mode of its enforcement, such as has lately become law in America.

We venture to think, however, that the simple record of the working of the *lex talionis* in individual cases, which our prison experience enables us to bring before our readers, may tend to show that the theories on which the capital penalty is founded and maintained do not always hold good when confronted with the stern reality of actual facts.

Before entering on this comprehensive theme, we must ask leave to make a personal explana– tion, like a maligned member of Parliament, in the shape of a strong protest against the charge that we are actuated by motives of "benevolence" in any statements we may make which suggest a doubt as to the righteousness or wisdom of the death penalty.

No sooner does any one presume to write or speak in any way against this irremediable punishment, than they are immediately stigmatized as "benevolent" persons,—that courteous term being merely a thin disguise for the conviction that they are weak–minded idiots, who give all their pity to bloodthirsty murderers, and are blandly indifferent to the fate of the murdered.

Prison visitors see too much of crime in its worst aspect to be capable of false benevolence, or to have the smallest desire that assassins should escape the direst penalty which can be awarded to them for their cruel deeds; but we cannot be blind to the facts bearing on the administration of the law in all its phases, which are brought into strong relief by the true histories we have to tell. These facts may be left to speak for them– selves, as the subject is assuredly not one in which there is any room for private fancies, or for the indulgence of an unreasoning sentimentality; but we will briefly enumerate some of the difficulties respecting capital punishment which they seem most forcibly to illustrate. We may instance, first, the inequalities and actual failures of human justice in meting out a penalty that can never be revoked, even if proved to have been mistakenly awarded to the innocent. This argument was very comprehensively stated by Lafayette when he declared that he would oppose the death decree until the **infallibility** of human judgment could be demonstrated to him; and the position was to some extent borne out, we think, by the history, already given in these pages, of a man who was executed for the wilful murder of the woman he most desired, above all others, to preserve in life. Our experience has also brought to our knowledge certain most startling revelations on the subject of the miscarriage of justice, which we shall endeavour in these pages to bring, at least to some extent, to the light of day.

For the present, however, the true stories we have to relate will be found to bear mainly on our conviction that capital punishment is not a deterrent of crime, but rather in some strange instances the reverse; that it is not the punishment most dreaded by criminals; and further, that it is not necessary or even conducive to the public safety.

Within a very short time after Ted Brown, the human gorilla, had passed from our prison to the realms unseen, a man, whom we will call John Butler, was brought to it on a charge of wilful murder. His personal appearance was very unlike that with which an assassin is usually credited—there was nothing in the slightest degree cruel or sinister in the expression of his countenance, which was on the contrary remarkably gentle and pleasant. He was a handsome fair–haired man, tall and strong, in the very prime of life. He gained his living at a lucrative trade, and had always occupied a position of great respectability in his native town, where he was much esteemed and beloved by numerous friends and relations. Butler had married at an early age, and with his young wife and four fine children, to whom he was deeply attached, he led a happy, peaceful life for several prosperous years. Then suddenly a dark shadow fell on the brightness of his days, the fiat came to him as to Ezekiel in the ancient time—"Behold, I take away from thee the desire of thine eyes with a stroke"—death entered into the midst of the little family in their pleasant cottage home, and took away the tender wife and mother, who was the source and centre of all their happiness. Butler followed her to her grave, half stupefied, and came back to look sorrowfully on his children—the youngest little more than an infant—and wonder what was to become of them while he was absent all day at his work; indeed, even if he had been able to stay at home, which as the bread–winner of the family was impossible, he would not have known how to care for them properly. A very poor expedient was resorted to for a time in the shape of a visit from his old mother, who reluctantly left her own household gods to come and indulge John's children in the most injudi- cious manner possible, and make abortive attempts with her failing eyesight to cook suitable dinners for them.

She found the little girls comparatively easy to manage, but the two boys, left to run wild, tormented her to the gradual extinction of her small stock of patience, and within a very few months the old woman struck work altogether, and declared she would have no more of it. She gathered up her small personal effects and went back to her own home, leaving John, as the *patois* of his native place expressed it, to "fend" for himself as best be could. Now John had an intimate friend, a very respectable man, generally supposed, we believe, to be gifted with great common–sense. This admirable quality he forthwith exercised on behalf of Butler, in a piece of advice which he was destined to expiate at a later period of his life in the bitterest regret and remorse: he solemnly counselled him to make a *mariage de convenance*—just such an alliance as in France is contracted between the son of a marquis and the daughter of a countess, from motives of the purest expediency, without any pretence of an attachment subsisting between them. John was personally not at all desirous to replace the dear wife he had lost, but he was ready to make any sacrifice on behalf of his children, whom he loved with a very unusual strength of affection. He answered his wise counsellor, therefore, by saying that he supposed it was the best plan he could adopt for the proper care of his little ones, only he did not know of any woman that would suit. His friend intimated that he did;—there was a certain single woman, robust and capable, living in the place, with apparently no family ties or encumbrances of any kind, who appeared to be very respectable, and likely to prove an excellent manager of a household. Butler might try her for a week or two in that capacity first, and if she proved efficient he had better marry her at once. It seems not to have occurred to this friend, in spite of his remarkable common–sense, that the fact of the woman living a long way apart from all her relations might indicate some strong peculiarity in her temper or disposition which made her absence from those bound to her, even by the ties of blood, an imperative necessity; nor did any such ominous thought pass through the mind of poor John himself. He meekly consented to follow his friend's advice, and annex this desirable female to his little kingdom if she were willing to become his second wife.

On that point the lady left no room for a moment's doubt. She closed with John's offer in so vehement and expeditious a manner as to suggest the probability that she looked upon it as her sole chance of matrimony.

Mainly by her strongly expressed will, the marriage was hurried on as quickly as possible, and the unfortunate John had literally no knowledge whatever of her character when he was summarily borne to the church, and there bound to her irretrievably till death should them part. On their return to John's house from the due performance of the ceremony,—at about that stage in the wedding festivities when in another rank of life the bridegroom is expected to rise to his feet and declare that it is the proudest and happiest day of his life,—the newly made Mrs Butler took her husband by the sleeve and led him into a corner apart from the guests, in order to make him a confidential communication: it was expressed in the following words—

"John Butler, now I have got you, **I'll** let you know what I am."

And she did let him know—during several years of unutterable wretchedness, which, in all that concerned the fate of his miserable children, may be said to have become absolute torture.

The woman his sensible friend had so obligingly recommended to him proved to have the temper of a fiend, and to be endowed also with certain other qualities which are supposed to be eminently characteristic of the denizens of an unmentionable region. Within ten days from the time of their marriage, she had, according to her promise, imparted to poor John such a remarkable knowledge of what she really was, that he went off in hot haste to the distant village where her parents lived, in order to ascertain, as far as possible, what her character and antecedents had really been. A terrible revelation was made to him there! He learned that no human being had ever been able to live with the woman; that she was malicious, cruel, and vindictive; and that her own father and mother had for their very peace and safety been compelled to dismiss her from their home and repudiate her altogether. Nevertheless, John Butler had taken her for better, for worse, and he had no alternative but to return to his own abode, and bear the curse he had brought upon his life as best he could. Then, in that cottage home where he had hitherto reigned as undisputed lord and master, there occurred a phenomenon—one not unknown to history certainly, but still surely a phenomenon! John Butler was, as we have seen, a man of extremely powerful *physique*, and his wife was a small wiry–looking woman of very insignificant appearance. Yet she managed in some inscrutable manner to acquire a despotic power and dominion over her husband, which reduced him to a condition of the most abject submission and slavery. How helplessly he writhed under her indomitable tyranny, was soon very sadly proved by his utter inability to shield even his children from her cruelty. It seemed incredible weakness on his part; yet he spoke of it to the writer as if he had been under a spell which bound him as in chains of iron. During the years which elapsed before he broke through his terrible bondage by a stroke that brought death to himself as

23

well as to her, he saw—first his youngest child—once a merry rosy—cheeked girl—done to death by ill—usage, and laid, a wasted, pallid little corpse, by the side of its true mother. Then he had to endure the sight of his eldest boy Harry, his especial favourite, and his only remaining daughter, a gentle young girl, being turned out of the house by their step—mother, and told that they were to darken her doors no more,—they might find a home and a living for themselves in any way they could. A lady consented to take the poor girl into her service, and the boy went to London, where he succeeded in getting only a very hard ill—paid situation, in which after—events proved that he had been exceedingly unhappy. There remained the younger boy, who earned a little money at his father's trade, and the woman therefore allowed him to remain at home; but she indemnified herself for this indulgence by systematically starving him. How she intended him to live without food has never been explained: the mode in which he actually received his necessary nourishment was by his father concealing certain portions from his own meals in a secret place known only to the boy, where he went to find them when he could succeed in eluding his step—mother's notice.

It may be imagined that during these miserable years the unhappy man often felt that he must free himself from his terrible tyrant by any means, right or wrong. He knew too little of legal processes to be aware that he might have sued for a formal separation; and even if he had known it, most probably the expense of such a proceeding would have been beyond his means. Anyhow, he did continue to endure his misery, although his wife gradually became a confirmed drunkard, and also, it is said, added to her other misdeeds by certain sins against her husband, for which, had he been a Turk resident in Constantinople, he might have openly tied her up in a sack and plunged her into the Bosphorus, with the entire approval of the public and all judicial authorities. The true gentleness and generosity of his nature were, however, shown on one occasion, when, by merely remaining passive, he might have got rid of his incubus for ever. In a fit of drunkenness the woman suddenly attempted to destroy herself, and Butler's little son one day ran to tell him that his step—mother had hung herself in the cellar. The man instantly rushed to the place, cut the rope which held her, carried her tenderly up—stairs in his arms, and by the most strenuous exertions succeeded in restoring her to the life that was not yet extinct. This was certainly a sufficient proof that no premeditated idea of violence towards her had entered into his mind.

About a fortnight before the day when John Butler was brought handcuffed between two policemen to the prison, he had one morning received a telegram from London, vaguely stating that his boy Harry had committed suicide, but with no details as to the circumstances under which the tragedy had taken place. Now Harry had only left his father's house the day before, having been allowed to go home from his situation for a very short holiday. What might have occurred there to drive him to quench his own young life is not known, but the act was very significant. Butler was almost beside himself with distress at this terrible news respecting his favourite son, and wished to start instantly for London to learn what had really occurred; but his determined tyrant peremptorily stopped him from doing anything of the kind. She intimated that he was to stay at home and attend to his work, while she herself would go to London to investigate the matter, and at the same time pay a visit to her sister who resided there. She coerced the unfortunate man into submitting to this arrangement, and departed. Of course he expected to hear from her immediately; but for three days she left him in his cruel suspense without any tidings from her whatever. At last she sent merely a vague telegram saying that the inquest on his son was over, with the usual verdict; and then, half maddened by his continued uncertainty as to the cause and manner of his poor boy's death, Butler took the next train to London, and went first to the house of his sister–in–law, where he believed his wife to be. She was not there, nor had she slept in the house at all. Where was she, then? The woman was compelled to admit that her sister had spent the time, when she was supposed to be inquiring into the death of her step–son, in a disreputable house, drinking and otherwise indulging her peculiar tastes.

For ten days after that date Butler remained in his cottage, to which both he and his wife had returned, maintaining an imperturbable silence,—while he struggled fiercely with the storm of resentment and intolerable misery that raged within him. A touch must have opened the flood–gates of his almost uncontrollable wrath at any time; and at length the fatal moment came.

He returned home from his work one day, tired and wretched, and fell asleep before the fire. He had that morning sold some of his possessions, probably requiring in that way to meet the unusual expenses his poor boy's death had brought upon him; and when he woke, he found that his wife had rifled his pockets of the money thus acquired. and had gone out to spend it in the public–house. After he had ascertained this he returned to his place, and sat there silent and immovable. There seems to have fallen on his spirit in that terrible hour a darkness that might be felt—an utter hopelessness—a conviction that his life–agony had become unendurable,—who could gauge the intense bitterness of the pain that held him as in a vice? His daughter came in to see him just then for a few minutes, and to her he spoke quietly and kindly. She was soon followed by her step–mother, who instantly began to taunt him about the suicide of his beloved son, in terms so cruel and revolting that the young girl told the writer afterwards, she felt as if she could herself at that moment have killed the woman who was casting such vile aspersions on her dead brother. Child–like she thought only of escaping from the sound of those horrible words, and she went away, leaving her father alone with the deadly enemy of his children. What passed during the next fateful moments can never be fully known, though it is a significant fact that when Butler was next seen he had a fresh wound on his face as if some assault had been made upon him; but it is certain in any case, that the pent–up exasperation and misery of all the past years culminated then and there in one instant of blind unreasoning passion, which drove him to snatch up a knife from the table and put an end to the woman's life and his own agony with one swift stroke.

Where, in the sudden madness of that white heat of ungovernable rage, was there any room for the supposed deterring influence of the death penalty on murder? If the hangman and his rope had been facing him at the moment, it would have made no difference to the frantic impulse which goaded him to avenge the wrongs of his children and himself with a single fierce blow. When John Butler came to his right mind and saw what he had done, he went and called for his next–door neighbour to be a witness against him, and then calmly gave himself up to justice so soon as the police could be brought on the scene.

The popular sympathy on behalf of this man was widespread and deep; even his wife's own sister and other relations declared to the writer, that all their compassion was for him, and not for the unprincipled woman who had driven him to madness. In prison his demeanour was uniformly gentle and humble, and he manifested unbounded gratitude for the simple fact that no one molested him or spoke any harsh or cruel words, which seemed to him, in comparison with his home life, to be extraordinary kindness.

Moreover, his repentance, as in the sight of God, for his one moment of fatal anger, was profound and genuine. He told the writer, with tears streaming from his eyes, that he repented of his crime with all his heart and soul, and was prepared to expiate it to the uttermost. He had not the smallest wish to live, he said—only he felt for his children!—worse than motherless so long, and now fatherless! Sobs choked his utterance. He wrung his visitor's hand in a passionate grasp, and tried to stammer out words of blessing on any who would care for his children.

Scenes from a Silent World

The day of Butler's trial came, and he took his place in the dock. The counsel engaged to defend the prisoner devoted himself to the case with the utmost earnestness, and with much skill and talent but on account of some legal technicality, rather incomprehensible to ordinary mortals not learned in Blackstone and other authorities, it was considered undesirable to bring forward any witnesses as to the provocation the man had received. Practically, therefore, the evidence simply went to prove the self—evident fact of the murder, and the attempt to reduce it to manslaughter failed. The judge's charge said nothing of extenuating circumstances; and the jury were, with extreme reluctance, compelled to pronounce the man guilty. They accompanied their verdict with a strong recommendation to mercy, of which the judge took no notice whatever.

The dramatic effect of the scene at the moment when the sentence was pronounced was very striking. His lordship was a small elderly gentleman, whose appearance, so far from being imposing, was somewhat ludicrously feminine in his red gown and grey wig. Sitting in his chair, he leant forward on his cushioned desk, and facing the powerful, fine—looking man who stood before him, and who could easily have flung him aside with a movement of his strong hand, he composedly doomed him to be hanged by the neck till he was dead; and further informed him that his body was to be buried in the precincts of the prison.

John Butler heard his sentence standing motionless, with head erect. Only once during the whole course of the trial had his self—command given way, and that was when allusion was made to the suicide of his son: then tears burst from his eyes, and his broad chest heaved with smothered sobs; but it was only for a moment. He speedily regained his composure; and as he turned to leave the dock, he calmly waved his hand in token of farewell to some of his friends in the crowded court, who on hearing his sentence had given vent to their feelings in piteous cries and exclamations.

It so happened that very soon after the capital penalty had been adjudged to John Butler for the murder of his wife, a man was tried in London for precisely the same crime, and we copy from the official report of the case the sentence pronounced on him. In this instance, although the woman was effectually killed, it had been permitted that the deed should be entitled manslaughter. The judge described the provocation the man had received from his wife, and then said that "the prisoner seemed, in a paroxysm of rage, to have inflicted injuries upon her which caused her immediate death. He had indeed been guilty of manslaughter; but he could not bring himself to pass a longer sentence upon the prisoner than that of a term of imprisonment, the result of which was that he would be discharged." The term of imprisonment to which he was sentenced being, we believe, less than the time he had spent in jail awaiting his trial, the practical result of the punishment awarded to him was, that he left the court at once a free man, entirely exempt from any legal consequences of his crime.

We do not for a moment doubt that the judges who tried these two cases were both men of the highest principle and integrity, conscientiously desirous of performing their onerous duties to the very best of their power; but they differed in opinion and disposition, as units of the human race are wont to differ, and the consequence was, that to the one criminal was awarded life and honourable liberty, while to the other was given death, with irremediable disgrace on the children who survived him. We would venture merely to ask whether it is well that the lives of our fellow–creatures should be dependent on peculiarities of temperament in her Majesty's judges?

The law—or rather the State—had not yet done its worst for John Butler: a further penance was decreed for him, which according to the legal code in America would there have been wholly impossible. The man had been recommended to mercy; and as the circumstances which had led to his crime were well known—(some not very scrupulous persons even affirming that he had done right in ridding the world of such a being)—it was confidently expected that the sentence would not be carried into effect. Nevertheless strenuous efforts were made to ensure this result. A petition was sent to the Home Office from Butler's native town, which was signed literally by almost the whole population; another went from the city where the trial had taken place, endorsed by the most distinguished names belonging to it, including one very eminent legal authority; and lastly, the jury forwarded an appeal of their own, signed by every one of the twelve men, good and true, who had been unwillingly compelled by the machinery of the law to pronounce the word "guilty;"—and no one doubted that such an array of petitioners united in opposition to the execution of the sentence would prevail.

It had been impossible to conceal these efforts from the prisoner himself. His children and other near relations were allowed to visit him, and they naturally told him what had been done, and gave him the further information that a preliminary answer had been received from the Home Office, which stated that the prisoner's case, with the appeals made on his behalf, were under consideration. After that, no doubt was felt by most that Butler would be reprieved; and this opinion received strong confirmation from the fact, that nearly the whole of the short period alloted to criminals between their trial and execution had passed away, before the decision of the State authority as to his life or death was made known. Then the answer came—the law was to take its course; he was to die,—early on the second morning after the letter reached the prison. Little more than forty hours was granted to this man to prepare for his dreadful doom.

This is no unusual circumstance in connection with the infliction of the capital penalty. Whenever a criminal has been recommended to mercy, and there is a further appeal for his life in consideration of extenuating circumstances, the decision of the Home Secretary is almost invariably delayed till within a day of the execution, and the inadequate space of time thus allotted to a preparation for the dread mystery of death, has been repeatedly brought into notice in the public papers by prison chaplains and others.

A law has recently been passed in America which deals with the whole subject of capital punishment, and a good deal of interest attaches to some of its more important enactments as compared with our English customs; but we may here transcribe the clause which defines the due interval of preparation to which every criminal has a right, in face of his irreversible doom:—

From section 491 of the Code of Criminal Procedure of the State of New York.

"When a defendant is sentenced to the punishment of death, the judges holding the court at which the conviction takes place must make out . . a warrant . . . appointing a week within which sentence must be executed."

(Section 492.) "The week so appointed must **begin not less than four weeks**, and not more than eight weeks, after the sentence."

The rule in England, even in cases where there is no doubt that the sentence will be carried out, allows three Sundays only to intervene between the trial and the execution—so that if a man is tried on a Saturday, he has very little more than a fortnight allowed him to prepare; but where there is hope of a reprieve, the delay of the announcement that the man is to die, till within a few hours of his execution, not only adds a torturing element to his punishment which he has not legally incurred, but it limits the time of his real preparation to the one last agitating day when his friends come to take a final leave of him. The matter is not one of minor importance, as was keenly felt, we believe, by the saintly Abbé Croze, the chaplain of La Roquette in Paris, who ministered to all the culprits who during a period of twenty–five years expiated their crimes on the guillotine. The French system of leaving a man in complete ignorance of the time when his execution is to take place until the fatal hour actually arrives, told very heavily against that good priest's efforts to bring such criminals as Tropman, Avignoin, and Billoir to a fit state of preparation for their entrance on the dread eternity. The strange laxity of French prison discipline allowed some of these men to be engaged in playing cards with their jailers till within a few hours of their death; but it may be doubted whether the more decent provisions of our English custom, which dedicates a condemned man's last day to farewell interviews with his friends, can avail to render that brief space of time sufficient for the heavy responsibilities with which it is weighted.

In the case of poor John Butler, who was passionately beloved by his children and brothers, it was spent in all the agony of mind which the sight of their uncontrollable distress could not fail to awaken in him. One of his brothers was an invalid helplessly crippled, and as he looked up at the tall powerful man glowing with health and vigour, who was some years younger than himself, he exclaimed impetuously—

"John, John! I wish to heaven they would let me die instead of you! You might have a long life before you still—strong and hearty as you are, and fit for good work wherever you might be; and here am I but a useless burden on my family,— I'd go to the gallows for you willingly if they'd only let me!"

"No, Richard, no! I would never consent to that," said the doomed man, pressing his brother's hand; "it is I alone must suffer, for it is true that I did the deed, and it was very wrong and cruel—it was done in a moment of madness, when I was quite beside myself, and no one on earth knows what I had suffered till I was fairly driven out of my senses. They made no account of that at my trial; but I can tell you this, my life at home was rendered such a hell upon earth, that I have felt quite happy and peaceful since I have been here away from it all, though the time has been spent in a jail, with the sentence of death hanging over me."

John Butler's singularly affectionate disposition became strongly manifest in the few last hours allowed him by the State after his death–warrant arrived. It was with difficulty that his children were torn from his arms, and he could scarcely bear to lose sight even for a moment of the chaplain, to whom he had become strongly attached. His last messages on his way to the scaffold next morning were for those who had shown him sympathy and kindness. Thus every instant of his brief interval *in articulo mortis* was saturated with the influence of his strong earthly affections; and it must have been wellnigh impossible for him to turn his dying eyes from the beloved faces he should see no more, in order to look into the mysterious darkness of the unknown state that awaited him beyond these farewell hours.

Since it is no part of the law that a criminal should be kept in ignorance as to his doom till within a few hours of its accomplishment, and the matter is entirely dependent on the will of one State official, it is to be hoped that the strong representations already made on the subject may produce a change, at least in this particular, as regards the treatment of prisoners.

The story of John Butler is a very clear illustration of the truth which, as we have already said, has been forcibly demonstrated to us in our visits to the Silent World—that the capital penalty is not a deterrent of crime. We shall give in a future chapter the history of a very singular case, in which the prospect of death following at once on a murder, seemed to have been one of the motives for its commission by a most unhappy man; but for the moment we are only concerned to show that this portion of the penal code in our country has no real effect in the prevention of deeds of violence.

There is one factor in the inducements to crimes of this description, as regards the weaker sex, which has a force that dominates their whole being, to the exclusion of any other influence whatever—and that is the uncontrollable passion which often takes possession of a woman for the man who is her lover.

Where there is no moral or religious principle to produce self–restraint, as is generally the case among the uneducated classes, the hopeless abandonment of a woman with all her natural affections and impulses to this one overpowering sentiment, is often a very remarkable spectacle. Some time previous to the death of John Butler, that same prison held within its silent walls a young woman who had been condemned to death for the murder of her only child. At the time when she was seen by the writer, there was no reason to doubt that the sentence would be carried out; though ultimately it was found that her condition of health formed a legal obstacle to her execution, and her sentence was commuted to that of penal servitude for life. A visit was paid to her when only a short interval remained before the day which, according to the law, was to be her last.

Scenes from a Silent World

When the door of the condemned cell was opened, and she was first seen, she had no idea that any hope of reprieve could exist—there had been no recommendation to mercy in her case, and she believed herself irrevocably doomed to suffer the extreme penalty. All that she said, therefore, was uttered with the black shadow of death shrouding her from any participation in the living world, and thus giving a strange significance to the burning words in which she told her history.

Judging by her appearance, it would have seemed impossible that she could be capable of any act of violence whatever. She was young and fair, with delicate features and large blue eyes—her flaxen hair drawn round her head, and leaving exposed a face of waxen whiteness, set in the patient calm of despair. She was placed on the one seat which the cell afforded, quite unoccupied, with her hands folded in her lap. She looked like a meek and harmless young girl, and she spoke in a soft low tone, with no emotion apparent in her voice.

"Yes, I have got to die," she said, when some gentle allusion was made to her sad position. "I know that quite well, but it is not a matter of any consequence **now**."

She appeared to lay great stress on that last word, and then remained silent, but gradually the expression of her visitor's compassion and desire to serve her broke through the cold apathy in which she seemed plunged, and she manifested at last an eager desire to tell her whole story to her hearer. It was evident that it would be the greatest relief to her to do so, for she had already passed many days in the regulation silence of prison discipline, and she had found no vent for the memories and thoughts that were for ever curdling round her heart in its sleepless agony.

"Let me tell you how it has all been with me," she said, flinging out her hands as in a despairing appeal; and while she spoke with rapid eager utterance, her whole appearance became transformed by the passionate excitement of feeling which caused her to live again in the days that were past. The pale, half–insensible statue she had looked when first seen, appeared to spring into vivid burning life, that flamed in the sudden brightening of her great blue eyes, and sent a crimson flush to her white cheeks.

"Listen!" she cried—"I will tell you all. I was a poor wretched creature, with no one to care for me or wish me any good. I had been betrayed and left with an infant on my hands when I was little more than a child myself, in ignorance and helplessness. Then in all my misery I met **him**, the one who is all the world to me, and he said he loved me—do you hear?—he loved me! and he offered me to come and live with him always, and he would take care of me and make me happy, and give me all my heart's desire; but oh! my heart's desire was for him and him alone! he was so kind, so good, and grand to look upon, there was no one like him in the world for goodness and beauty, and I just adored and worshipped him. I can't find words to tell you how I loved him—there are no words that could tell it: he was my treasure, my joy, my king. I'd have laid down my life for him a thousand times over if he had asked it. A look, a whisper from him was enough to make me do anything he pleased; and I was happy—oh, how happy!"

She stopped for a moment to dash away the passionate tears which the remembrance of her past happiness had evoked, and then went on in a lower tone. "There was just one trouble—the child. It had grown to be some years old, and he hated it—he always did from the very first. I hid it away from him as much as I could, and it was easy while it was still a baby; but when it could run about and call me mother, he saw it and heard it, and he grew to detest it so, that he said he could not endure it in the house any longer. He had threatened me many times that if I did not get rid of it he'd leave me; but I could not believe at first he really meant it. I was willing enough to be quit of the child; for I could not think of it at all when I had him. I had given all my love and heart and soul to him, and he filled my whole life. There was no room for any other—not even the child I had borne. There came a day when it had angered him more than ever before, I don't know why. He was going away for a night to a town at a distance, and when he was ready to start he came to me. He put his two hands on my shoulders, and fixed his eyes on mine, and looked stern and fierce as I had never seen him. 'Now, understand,' he said, 'I'll have no more delay. You must take that cursed child away while I am gone, and leave it where I can never set eyes on it again, or else all will be at an end between you and me. I tell you plainly, if I find that child here when I come back to—morrow, I will leave you then and there, as sure as there's a sun in heaven, and I'll never look on your face again, or have anything more to do with you as long as you live.' He pushed me away from him and went out, but I rushed after him and flung my arms round his neck and cried out, 'Don't—don't say you'll leave me—I can't bear it; Ill do what you wish—I'll find a place for the child—I'll take it away,—only don't leave me—never, never!' 'See you do it, then,' he said; 'take the brat to the workus and have done with it.' He went away, and I had no thought but to make sure that he'd not leave me, whatever it might cost me to keep him with me. I knew it was no use to take the child to the workus, for I had tried that before; but they would not take it unless I'd go in too and stay in the house myself altogether.

That would have been worse than death to me, as it would have parted me from him. I never gave the workus another thought. That evening after he was gone, and I knew he'd be back next morning, and would leave me for ever if he found the child still there, I do not think I rightly knew what I was going to do; only I took it in my arms and walked with it as quickly as I could towards the river. When I got to it, there was not a creature to be seen far or near, and it was nearly dark. All the way as I went I had seemed to hear his voice saying over and over that he'd never see my face again, and it goaded me on, and left me no power to choose. The sound of his words came so loud, just when I got to the river, that I rushed down to the edge as if I had been driven by some one at my back; and then,—oh, to think of it!"

Suddenly a spasm of pain passed across the woman's face, and she put her hands over her ears as if to shut out some torturing echo from the past, to which yet her blanched, quivering lips were constrained to give utterance. "Then," she whispered hoarsely, "the child said to me, 'Oh, mother! don't put me in the dark water.' Yes, he did—he did—"and her voice rose to a shriek. It was evident that this dreadful remembrance scorched her very heart, and drove her to put into audible words the piteous cry that haunted her night and day. "Yes, he said that—my child did; but I only cried out—'I can't part with my love for ever,' and I let the little one drop out of my arms into the deep rushing river. The moment it was done, I would have snatched it out if I could, but the stream carried it away, and I saw it no more." She let her head fall down to her very knees, and crouched there in the grasp of an intolerable agony.

Presently she lifted up her convulsed face, and said with a bitter withering smile, "Do you know what was the end of it? As I walked home I met a woman who had seen me go out with the child in my arms, and she was one who knew well how he hated it. She asked me where it was, and what I had done with it. I said I had left it with a friend; and she answered, 'Yes, a fine sort of a friend, I expect;' and she went straight away to the police. That was a kind neighbour, was it not? They took me that same night, and locked me up,"—then she broke into a wild despairing cry, as she exclaimed—"I've never seen him since. His words came true, for all I gave up my child so cruelly, only to keep him with me—to be near him—my only love. We are parted now—parted for ever. I can't break down these walls to go to him. Oh, I hope they'll kill me soon! I can't live without him; let me die—let me die!"

Scenes from a Silent World

What deterring power had the thought of any ulterior consequences on this woman's crime? If this passion of love—"strong as death, and cruel as the grave,"—could overcome the laws of nature and the divine instincts of motherhood, it would certainly make no account of the worst that human laws could do, to avenge the guilt of its unbridled indulgence.

We had another instance once, in a very different case, of the extraordinary power which such indomitable affection has over the life and soul of a woman. There came into the prison on a trifling charge which did not involve a long detention, one of the most pitiable–looking beings it was possible to see,—a woman young in years, but haggard and wasted to the last degree, and with a great gaping wound, still open, on her forehead, which seemed to have been caused by a blow from a hatchet. She made no difficulty in explaining how she had received this serious injury; it had been done by her lover, with whom she had lived some years, though he was not her husband.

"He has a terrible temper," she said; "the least thing puts him in a fury, and then it's always on me he takes revenge. He has brought me nigh to death's–door many a time; and I know very well that he'll kill me in the end. I know he will."

She went on to give further details of the utter misery in which she lived. The man spent all his earnings in drink, and starved her. She toiled beyond her strength to gain a little money for food, and when she came home after a hard day's work, he snatched her wages from her, and went off to the public–house. Then when he came back, he beat her because she had not got a supper provided for him. There seemed no possible element of attraction in the life she led with him, even apart from the certainty which was ever present in her mind, that he would compass her death at last—some destined day. Yet when the visitor, anxious to rescue her from the sin and wretchedness of such an existence, offered to provide for her entirely if she would leave the miscreant to whom she was not bound by any righteous tie, she only lifted up her hollow mournful eyes, and said, "I will never leave him—never!"

Finally, in answer to the strong remonstrances made to her on the ground at once of the guilt and the misery of her life, she answered that she knew it was all true. She suffered night and day, she owned, from hunger and pain and ill–usage, and she could not even pray to God to help her, because of her sin. She knew she would be murdered in the end, and she supposed her soul would be lost, but still—"I cannot leave him—I will not—never, never—though you offered me to live in the Queen's palace: I'll go back to him the moment I am free, and I'll stay with him to the last hour of my life, however it may end,"—and she did. The utmost efforts to shake her resolution availed nothing—no human power could cope with the might of her passion for her destroyer; and she went back to him, saying that she would rather die by his hands than live without him.

The conviction that no case is absolutely hopeless, no criminal, however guilty, altogether im– pervious to good influences, is that which mainly sustains those who have to work among the inmates of a prison; but the instance we have just recorded was undoubtedly an exception to the rule—it was literally impossible to help the woman in any way. She would not abandon the fascination which held her as in bonds of iron, even to save her own life; and it is certain that no dread of legal penalties would have deterred her from any crime her tyrant had willed her to commit.

The instances we have as yet recorded of the working of the *lex talionis* in individual cases, apply only to those arguments in its favour which concern the policy and expediency of its enforcement in relation to the practical results; but there are other and far deeper principles involved in its theoretic position as a righteous enactment of the law, which must sooner or later be thoroughly investigated in the light of a more advanced civilisation than that of the days when the death penalty was left to be the punishment of one especial crime, even while happily banished from the code of lighter offences. On those weightier matters we have yet to speak; but meanwhile, we earnestly trust that the readers of these pages may share our conviction—that the whole subject we have so far endeavoured to elucidate by the painful histories we have given is of far more serious importance than appears on the surface. Many wise persons among our legislators, and others, are of opinion, judging by the signs of the times, that the lower stratum of society, from which the criminal classes are recruited, may at some future period, more or less distant, become a great, perhaps a dominant, power in the kingdom. Surely, therefore, it would be well, while there is yet time, that a careful consideration should be given to such portions of the existing legal code as may seem to them to savour of injustice or oppression. An eminent counsel speaking recently in defence of a prisoner, stated openly that various important changes in the administration of justice were already in contemplation by the authorities. We trust, therefore, that such light as these scenes from prison life can cast on the subject will prove to be not ill–timed.

CHAPTER III. THE ACQUITTAL OF A MURDERER.

"Then though our foul and limitless transgression
Grow in our growth and in our breath began,
Raise Thou the arms of endless intercession,
Jesus! divinest when Thou art most man."**IT** is to be hoped, judging by the present state
of feeling on all that concerns the welfare of the people, that the best and wisest modes of
dealing with the criminal classes will really become one of the great questions of the day.
Such a result is much to be desired, especially if the attention of those who are in a
position to influence the Legislature can be drawn to the subject in detail. A conviction
has been growing up of late in the minds of many persons who take an interest in the
outcasts of the population, that our prisons ought to be made more productive of moral
benefit to their inmates than is the case at present. The impression, indeed, is very
general, that prisoners—male and female alike—often come out of jail worse than they
were when they went in,—that they encounter there an actively deteriorating influence,
and acquire—at least the younger criminals—a greater knowledge of evil than they had
attained in their previous career. Those who form their opinion only outside the prison
walls, or after a brief official visit, are not, however, in a position to judge rightly on
these points; it requires a long and intimate acquaintance, both with the criminals
themselves and with the machinery which surrounds them, to gauge adequately the nature
and extent of the problems involved in the legal administration of punishment.

So far as a ten years' experience with these advantages may be trusted, we are decidedly
of opinion that the risk of evil influences to a prisoner within the jail has been greatly
overrated.

It is a rigid rule in all penal establishments that the inmates are not to be allowed the
smallest intercourse among themselves. Such communication, therefore, as they do
succeed in holding with each other, is obtained surreptitiously by means of much
ingenious trickery, and it is too circumscribed and dangerous to admit of any elaborate
tutoring of the younger prisoners in crime. It frequently happens, also, that some sparks
of latent good feeling in the minds of the older and more hardened criminals, lead them to
look with a certain sorrowful pity on the immature aspirants to their craft; and they are
more inclined to warn them of its miserable results than to guide them into its lower

depths.

While, however, we are disposed to deny, generally speaking, the existence of any active agencies for evil within the jail, we freely admit that unless strong measures are taken for the improvement and moral education of the prisoners, it is likely that they will undergo a passive deterioration, during the long solitary hours spent in sullen brooding in their cells over the crimes of the past and the possibilities of the future. As the prison system is at present constituted, we do not hesitate to say that the remedial means provided are inadequate for the purpose. These consist for the most part solely of the duties devolving on the prison chaplains. We cannot speak too highly of that admirable body of men. Those whom we have been fortunate enough to know intimately, have been absolutely devoted to their onerous duties, and have done all that human beings can do under the circumstances. But if a single solitary man is set in face of a large number of criminals, succeeding each other more or less rapidly, as their sentences are long or short, and is told that it is his business to bring them one and all from darkness into light, it is physically impossible that, even with the sacrifice of his whole life, he can really accomplish what he is supposed to undertake. In the case of the female prisoners he has a special difficulty of a most formidable kind. According to a stringent rule which obtains in all convict establishments of every description, the chaplain is not allowed to see the women alone—a female warder has to be present during all his interviews with them, even when they are sick or dying in the jail infirmary. This rule is not only right, but rigorously necessary for the protection of the clergyman himself from the false statements which would infallibly be made respecting him by the lawless and utterly reckless beings with whom he has to deal, were no witnesses present at his interviews with them; but we need scarcely say that it renders his ministrations among them almost entirely fruitless. He can never gain their confidence, or hear the truth from their lips, while they are conscious of being watched by a prison official.

Admitting, then, that the measures at present adopted for the moral and religious improvement of the prisoners are out of all proportion to the object it is desired to attain, there seems to be only one remedy that could meet the necessities of the case—and that is a regular system of visitation by volunteers from without, who, under the direction of the governor and chaplain, should co-operate with them in efforts for the reformation of the criminal.

That such extraneous help is a distinct necessity in the case of the female prisoners, for the reason we have given above, seems to have been to some extent recognised by the Prison Commissioners, as lady visitors have now been appointed for the women in a few of the principal jails of the kingdom. The number is as yet, however, very small where such additional help is afforded, and we are not aware that it has been extended in any instance to the male prisoners.

There would be one advantage in the admission of supernumerary workers to prisons, which might not occur to the minds of those interested in the subject, but which is none the less a very cogent reason for their employment,—it lies in the fact that they would be **unpaid** volunteers, known by the prisoners not to be in receipt of an official salary as an equivalent for their labours among them. We can best prove the truth of this statement by giving a brief account of a prisoner, whose history was also in other respects somewhat remarkable.

This man had been in prison for a considerable time, and only two months of the term to which he had been sentenced remained to be gone through, when he became very ill with what was pronounced to be pulmonary consumption. He was passed into the infirmary ward, and there he came under the notice of the visitor attached to that jail. The account given of him, previous to his failure in health, was extremely unsatisfactory. When he first entered the prison to await his trial, he had not only refused to give his name, but said in the most determined manner that none should ever know who he was or where he came from, or anything whatever concerning him. If they must have a name whereby to designate him in the prison records, they might take Jack Smith—it would do as well as any other. During the whole time of his imprisonment after conviction, he maintained the same obstinate silence as to his antecedents,—in fact, his demeanour was characterised by an unvarying sullenness, and he never opened his lips to any one unless he were compelled. The chaplain did his best with him, but he certainly could never have had a more hopeless subject for his ministrations. The man was not openly rude or insolent, as he knew that such conduct could only bring down condign punishment upon himself; but he took care to make it distinctly evident that when the clergyman tried to instruct or admonish him, he deliberately fixed his mind on some thoughts of his own, so as to avoid even hearing the words which were addressed to him; and he never made the slightest response of any kind. In chapel, it is the defiant custom of prisoners who, like himself, have no desire to share in the services, to stand like soldiers on parade, the arms hanging straight by the side, the eyes fixed on the wall, and the lips firmly closed, as if the singing of the hymns and chants were as meaningless to them as the moaning of the wind outside the narrow windows. It seemed plain that the chaplain's visits served only to confirm him in his dogged reserve and silence. Several other convictions were recorded against him, and the opinion held of him by the authorities was clearly expressed in one brief sentence addressed by the governor to the visitor who asked to see him—

"You can go to him, of course, if you like, but you had better understand at once that he is a thoroughly bad fellow in every way, without a redeeming point about him."

He received his visitor in perfect silence, and his aspect at first sight was certainly not encouraging—a gaunt, haggard–looking man lying motionless in bed, with his eyes dark and keen as those of a hawk, fixed on the one narrow window high up in the wall, through which a strip of blue sky could be seen—his breathing hurried and feverish, and his large wasted hands, where the bones stood out like those of a skeleton, clenched every now and then as if some secret thought moved him to sudden anger.

On this first occasion the visitor turned the conversation entirely to the state of his health, promising to obtain from him, with the doctor's permission, the means of alleviating the thirst which consumed him, and showing all possible sympathy with his physical sufferings. The prisoner answered very briefly; but towards the close of the interview he suddenly turned his eyes on his visitor with a long scrutinising gaze, which seemed to have some peculiar meaning. What that had been was explained next day, when the chief warder informed the visitor of a brief conversation he had held with the sick man the evening before. The prisoner had begged leave to ask a question: he wished to know whether the individual who had visited him that day was a paid official like the chaplain, so that any attention shown by that visitor to the convicts was simply the accomplishment of a routine duty necessarily performed as an equivalent for value received. The warder was somewhat indignant, and responded angrily that it was like his insolence to ask any such question: he might have been sure that the attendance at the prison of a person of that description was entirely voluntary, and that no payment ever could or would be made for it. The prisoner answered that he meant no offence; but he thought the officer might under– stand that it made all the difference in the world to himself and to every other prisoner, if they had to listen to a chaplain who was hired to preach to them, or to a person who came to them out of pure goodwill. Subsequent inquiries proved that this is a universal feeling on the part of criminals, who would scarcely have been expected to indulge in so refined a sentiment; but it certainly affords a strong reason for the employment of voluntary workers in addition to the regular officials.

The information given on the subject to this especial prisoner produced a remarkable change in his demeanour. When he next saw his visitor, though he was still a man of few words, he showed himself decidedly grateful and pleased at the attention paid to him; and towards the close of the interview he suddenly raised himself on his elbow, turned round and faced his visitor with a keen eager look, while he said—

"I want to know this—have you the least idea how bad I have been, and am? I won't have you deceived in me. I tell you I have been just as bad as a man can be, and I delighted in all my wickedness, and never wished to leave it off. I have done every wrong thing you could think of, excepting murder. I never got let in for that, or I'd have swung for it long ago; but it was a chance I didn't, for I never stopped at any crime that came in my way. You ought to know the truth if you are coming often to see me."

"I do know it," was the answer; "but it makes me only the more anxious to be a true friend to you."

"A friend!" he exclaimed—"a friend!" He remained silent for a few minutes with his piercing eyes staring into the face of his visitor, then he suddenly flung himself back on his pillows, muttering, "Well, when I came into this hateful place, ay, and long before, I thought I had done with friends for ever and ever! It goes very hard with me to believe I've got one now."

Nevertheless he did come to believe, not only in the sympathy of his visitor, but in the existence also of a Friend perfect in love and power, to whom he turned in all sincerity for pardon and peace before the termination of his life on earth.

The end came for him in a very singular manner. Far above all his remorse for the past, and the maddening recollection of certain dark episodes in his secret history, there was one dominant passion which had entire possession of his whole being, and that was the burning desire of liberty—the almost frantic craving to be free,—to escape from these stone walls which held him captive, from that closely barred window where the light of day was only granted in such niggard fashion to his longing eyes; from the resistless authority of his jailers, and from the very sound of those clanking keys which always pervades the atmosphere of a prison as unceasingly as the air of the sea-shore is filled with the perpetual moan of its waves;—if only—he used to sigh out—the long days and nights would pass more quickly, till that blissful hour should come when by law he must be liberated, when the iron gates would open wide and he would go forth! He counted the very moments he had yet to pass in durance, over and over again. "One day less, one night less, twelve hours less," he would exclaim triumphantly when his visitor came in, and soon only a week or so of the time remained. Nevertheless the doctor had grave doubts whether the man would live to go out. His malady was increasing with alarming rapidity, his strength ebbing away, and the symptoms of approaching dissolution becoming plainly visible,—yet it never seemed to occur to him that he could fail to obtain his release at the destined hour. He listened eagerly to the arrangements which, by his own wish, had been made for his removal, on the day when the term of his sentence was to expire. It came at last—a beautiful morning, so bright that even the high narrow window admitted a little ray of sunshine, which fell on the wan face of the prisoner as the visitor came to stand by his bedside. One glance was enough to show that the shades of death had already gathered there. He was silent and almost motionless, exhausted by the convulsive struggle for breath in which he had passed the night. If he still remembered that the day of his release had dawned, he knew also that he was about to obtain a more perfect liberty than ever he had dreamt of in all his longings—that the hour waited for with such passionate desire would render him, in the highest sense—free indeed! and so it was. The ceaseless prayer he had so long unconsciously made in the words of the Psalmist, "Bring my soul out of prison," was granted at last, and before the sun set on that appointed day, he had passed to the pure airs and boundless expanse of regions far beyond the confines of this mortal world. The dreary cell of his slow painful penance retained only the lifeless form that could suffer no more.

For the reasons illustrated by the above narrative, and many others, we are disposed, as we have said, to advocate strongly the employment of voluntary workers among the inmates of our prisons; but at the same time we are perfectly aware of the serious difficulties which stand in the way of such a scheme.

At present the rules against the admission of outsiders within the walls are most stringent, and it might seem as if any infringement of these enactments would be subversive of all proper discipline.

Apart from those few prisons where, of late years, lady visitors have been allowed to penetrate to the women's cells, no unofficial persons are ever allowed to pass the gates, except the relations of the prisoners themselves. These are permitted to have an interview with them once in three months. It is limited to twenty minutes, and takes place in the presence of a warder, the visitor standing outside the cell door, where a grating admits an imperfect view of the captive within, and allows his carefully guarded words to be heard by his friend and the officer in charge. No doubt it would be a great innovation on this disciplinary system to open the doors to unofficial persons, and allow them such free access to the prisoners as would be necessary to render their ministrations of real use. It must be owned, also, that there would be considerable difficulty in obtaining workers properly qualified for so peculiar a position; in fact, some among the lady visitors recently chosen have had to be summarily withdrawn, in consequence of injudicious proceedings. A sound judgment, and a high sense of honour as regards the slightest infraction of rule, with various other less conspicuous qualities, are imperatively required to form an efficient worker; and unhappily these are not often found in combination. For this reason, probably, the governors of prisons, generally speaking, so greatly dislike the idea of an invasion of unofficial visitors, that it is to be doubted if they would even welcome a select band of sensible angels, if such could be sent them, from the celestial hierarchy. Of course the office is one which involves many strange and unexpected perplexities: amongst others, we may mention that the visitor is apt to become the recipient of dangerous secrets. We can give an instance of this kind in a history, which is valuable also as illustrating the fallibility and uncertainty of human justice, to which we have alluded in some former records from the Silent World,

A man and his wife were sent to the prison with which the writer is connected, having been committed to take their trial for the alleged murder of a child. It had been the woman's own offspring, but was only step–son to the male prisoner. The facts brought out in evidence at the inquest were simply these: The man had been alone in an up–stairs room with the child when its death took place. The only other person in the house was his wife, the little one's own mother. She remained in the kitchen below, and did not go near the child till she was told by her husband that it was dead. A doctor was then sent for, although, of course, it was evident that his services could be of no avail. He stated at the inquest that all the indications, from the state of the child's head, pointed to murderous violence having been used against it; but he admitted that it was within the range of possibility that the fatal injuries it had sustained might have been caused by an accidental fall out of its little chair, which the step–father affirmed to have been the origin of the disaster. The coroner was of opinion that the case was one which ought to be brought under the searching investigation of a court of justice, and he therefore sent both the persons implicated to await their trial in prison. They had a younger infant, the legitimate child of the man, for which it seemed both had always shown a marked preference: it was left in the care of a neighbour.

The woman, who was young, timid, and weak, was in a state of nervous excitement which rendered her unceasingly restless, and she welcomed the visitor's interviews with her eagerly, as a relief from the monotonous solitude of her cell. She maintained at first a cautious reserve on the subject of the supposed crime, and of course her silence was respected. After a time, however, she ascertained that any statement made to the person who alone was allowed to converse with her, was always received in strict confidence—certain not to be reported to either prison authorities or magistrates; and further, that the visitor was not there to intervene in any way respecting either the crime or the punishment of prisoners, but only to offer them advice and consolation in the present, and such help as might be possible in the future. Being at last fully satisfied on this point, her reserve gave way, and one day, when she was more than usually depressed, she burst out with the whole truth as to the death of the child, giving every particular with a vehemence which the visitor had no power to check.

She began by explaining that the unfortunate little boy had been a source of discord and contention between herself and her husband ever since the birth of the infant which was legally his own; then without the least attempt to palliate the enormity of the act, she stated in so many words the terrible truth that he had indeed deliberately murdered him. She knew that he went to the room where the boy was for the purpose, and it seems almost incredible that she should have been so unnatural a mother as not to have even tried to protect her own child; but it is to be feared that she had no desire to do so. The only trace of feeling she showed while minutely describing the harrowing details we gladly withhold from our readers, was in the admission that she could not, as she expressed it, follow her husband up–stairs "to see it done!" By her passive connivance at the crime, she was of course virtually as guilty as the man himself. The full revelation of the murder thus made remained of neces– sity a secret, known to no single individual except the writer, who was present a little later at the trial of the accused persons.

It took place at the next assizes, and the first proceeding of the grand jury was to throw out the bill against the woman altogether. She was instantly discharged, and the man alone appeared in the dock.

The witnesses against him were few in number. His wife, of course, could not be examined, and the evidence was limited to that of the medical man who had been called in, and one or two neighbours, who could only testify generally as to unkind treatment towards the child on the part of the prisoner at the bar. The doctor's evidence was decidedly the most damaging, and it was plain that the accused man was painfully conscious of its weight and significance, for his face became ghastly with fear as he listened,—in his guilty consciousness he clearly believed himself doomed, and at least in that moment he did by anticipation taste the bitterness of death. It was easy to see what the doctor's private opinion was, and that he had not the smallest doubt a cruel murder had been committed, but he was bound only to speak as to facts; and under a severe cross–examination from the prisoner's counsel, he was compelled to admit that the circumstances were consistent with a possible accident, such as the man had from the first declared to have been the cause of the child's death.

After the evidence had been taken, and the counsel on both sides had made their speeches, the judge proceeded to sum up and deliver his charge to the jury. In the most eloquent and convincing manner possible, he proved to them that the man was, in the eye of the law, perfectly innocent of the crime which had been laid to his charge. There was no reliable evidence against him—no human eye had beheld the events which had resulted in the death of the child—not one person could testify that they had seen the step–father inflict any injury upon him on that occasion; they must dismiss from their minds what had been stated as to his harshness at other times—they were concerned only to inquire into the circumstances which had occurred on the one fatal day. It was a point strongly in the prisoner's favour, that he had himself gone instantly to bring a doctor to the scene (the child being safely dead, be it remembered). The medical gentleman had admitted that the accident described by the prisoner would account for the death, and in short the man must be pronounced innocent. In the words of the hymn—
"All his converse was sincere,
His conscience as the noonday clear." The jury, without even retiring from their box, brought in a verdict of "Not guilty." The accused man was honourably acquitted—discharged forthwith from the custody of the police, and in another moment he had hurried out of the court and disappeared.

One person who listened to the judge's "admirable summing up," as the newspapers termed it, and to the unanimous verdict, knew certainly that the man thus pronounced to be innocent had in truth been guilty of a most brutal premeditated murder; and it was impossible to escape the in– ference, that if the fallible human justice could thus dismiss an unmitigated villain with an honourable acquittal, it must be equally liable to an error of judgment in the opposite direction,—and an innocent man pronounced guilty of murder passes to a punishment which can never in this life be revoked.

Whatever may have happened in the past, the risk of so painful a mistake occurring in these days certainly lies in the possibility of perjury on the part of hostile witnesses. We believe that the danger of false evidence being tendered on oath in our courts of justice by persons of a certain class, is far from being sufficiently estimated by those in authority. It is part of the experience gained in the Silent World to gauge the depths of that utter disregard of truth in which children of the lowest class are nurtured from infancy upward, till, when they reach maturity, it has become a second nature. Where any vindictive feeling happens to be cherished against a prisoner, there is not the smallest scruple among such persons in swearing to the grossest falsehoods concerning him; and we have known instances where the love of notoriety alone, in the case of female witnesses, has produced the same result. The newspapers have quite lately been expatiating on the release of two innocent men from penal servitude in consequence of its having become known that the evidence given against them some years ago was false, and there has been commendable speed in sending them a free pardon for the crime they never committed. Fortunately for these poor men, their sentence was not of that irrevocable nature which would have rendered any such restitution impossible.

Prison visitors can often be of great use to criminals awaiting trial by inducing them to deal truthfully with their Counsels, and to act in all respects righteously as regards their offences against the law. It is one of the many channels open to them for the moral improvement of the unlucky denizens of the Silent World. As we desire strongly to advocate an organisation of voluntary workers for these purposes, it is only just that we should give some little insight into the difficult nature of the work in its various branches. The story we have just told shows that they are very likely to be made the recipients of dangerous secrets within the jail itself, but the possession of information from without involves an equally heavy responsibility.

One of the most rigid rules which officially appointed visitors have to obey, is that which prohibits them from conveying to the prisoners the smallest fraction of intelligence as to anything which may be taking place in the world outside the walls. They are thereby often landed in very perplexing positions. One of the most romantic histories revealed in our prison is connected with an instance of this kind. A very beautiful woman had, for some unknown reason, been transferred from London to the jail of which we have been writing. The offence which had brought her a year's imprisonment was one of which it was quite possible that she might have been as guiltless as she declared she really was. She affirmed that it was a case of mistaken identity. She was comparatively young, and even the unsightly convict dress could not hide the symmetry of her features or the grace of her movements. She had received a superior education, and was possessed of great musical talent. She had, we believe, been the *prima donna* of a London music–hall, and had been in the habit of singing there nightly to a charmed audience, with whom she was a favourite, and who often greeted her on her appearance with showers of bouquets. It was a dangerous position, especially for an attractive young woman, without either father or mother to protect her, and poor No. 19 bad not been proof against the allurements that beset her.

For a long time nothing whatever was known of her antecedents within the jail. She maintained as many prisoners do, an absolute reserve towards the officials, holding as little intercourse with them as was possible. Her conduct was exemplary so far as the regular routine of work and discipline was concerned, but it was believed that when she was shut into her cell for the night in solitude and silence, she often gave way to paroxysms of passionate weeping, beating herself against the stone walls that held her in such rigid bondage.

It happened that the visitor had been absent for a little time after No. 19 came to the prison, and therefore inquired, before a first interview with her, into the facts known respecting her; but the records of this case, when examined, contained no account whatever of the woman's previous history, so determinedly had she concealed it from all around her, and at first she maintained the same silence with her visitor. When a few interviews had taken place between them, however, she made the discovery that whatever confidence she gave to this person would be held inviolate; and then the pent–up longing to relieve the aching burden of unshared thought, and feel the touch of human sympathy which generally takes possession of prisoners during a lengthened incarceration, drove her to a full revelation of her life–history in the past and her hopes for the future. Hers had been an experience only too sadly common among women of her ardent and undisciplined nature; but there were certain circumstances connected with her position at the time which gave it an unusual interest. She had been educated more or less as a lady, but being left friendless at an age when her beauty and attractions were at their height, she was glad to turn her musical talents to account as a means of living, and became, as we have said, a public singer. The life of excitement, the gay and brilliant scenes in which she figured nightly, the applause with which she was always greeted, were full of fascination to her, and she was very happy in her somewhat dangerous career. Then she attracted the notice of a man whose name she would not at first reveal, even to the visitor whom she trusted, because she knew that it was familiar to every one as that of a person in a very high position, both socially and politically. After a time, during which he lavished upon her every proof of real affection he could bestow,—loaded her with precious gifts, and gave rise to no suspicion of evil intentions,—the usual miserable result followed: he persuaded her to go abroad with him under a promise of marriage, when certain obstacles which stood in the way should have been removed. She knew the error of such a course, and hated the consciousness of wrong–doing in herself, even if it were to be only temporary; but she could not resist the entreaties of the voice she loved, or the specious promises that accompanied them. It was simply another case of that blind unreasoning passion of a woman for her idol, which fills the prison books with some of the darkest crimes they have to record.

Her life had thus become one of luxury and splendour, spent as much as possible on the Continent, during which time the hope of marriage was probably ever before her, lending a very false colouring to her position. There were frequent intervals, however, when public affairs required that her companion should leave her; and it was during one of those periods of solitude that she was suddenly charged with the offence which ultimately brought her within the prison walls. According to her own account, not only was it a mere case of mistaken identity, but she was actually abroad at the time when she was supposed to have been committing a fraud in London: and this fact she declared to her visitor she could have proved instantly at her trial had she chosen to call as witness the gentleman who had been travelling with her there. But she knew that to do this would be to bring his well–known name into the papers, coupled with her own, in a disgraceful manner; and she preferred rather to endure the term of imprisonment which the undefended accusation brought upon her, than to injure fatally the reputation of the man she loved.

It is difficult to believe that a woman who had gone so far wrong as she had done, and was of so passionate and impulsive a nature, could have been capable of an act of generosity which was to bring a most galling punishment upon herself; but the writer saw a letter from her to the man in question, which undoubtedly bore out the truth of her statement. Perhaps such a generous act may have been rendered more easy for her by the hope it engendered, that her lover would reward her for it by accomplishing the long–desired marriage, all obstacles to which had, as it happened, been removed. She no longer withheld his name from the visitor, and it was evident that she brooded on the thought of him and of her possible future night and day. At the same time, she appeared to be strongly moved by the efforts of those who sought to influence her for good, and she promised to abide by their earnest advice, and to see this man no more unless he did in truth make her his wife. She gave some evidence of sincerity in her intentions by agreeing to remain under the visitor's care, after her release from jail, until it could be seen what her fate was likely to be, and the course which it would be right for her to adopt in accordance with it. Matters were in this position, and a considerable portion of her term of imprisonment still remained to be undergone, when the visitor one morning found a whole column of a London paper filled with an account of the magnificent wedding of the man in whom poor No. 19 had trusted so devotedly. Troops of aristocratic friends had surrounded him and the lady who held herself to be supremely fortunate in becoming his wife. An ecclesiastical dignitary had tied the knot, and crowds had waited outside the church to greet with acclamations the highly placed bridegroom who was supposed to have the interests of the people especially at heart.

We have told this story mainly to illustrate some of the perplexities which are apt to beset prison visitors in the discharge of their duties, and here was certainly a notable instance. The rule, binding persons appointed to that office never to bring tidings from the outside world to the knowledge of the prisoners under any circumstances whatever, rendered it impossible for the writer to give No. 19 the faintest hint of an event which must inevitably alter the whole course of her future life, and at once dispel the fervent hopes she had cherished so fondly. Naturally it became thenceforth extremely difficult to know how to counsel and support a woman who had to be kept in ignorance of that which was in fact the key–note of her destiny, and who must be left in her delusion to make plans which could never be realised.

There was no help for it, however. It might have been easy enough for the visitor to evade the rule in that particular instance without its ever becoming known to the authorities, but of course such a proceeding would have been simply dishonourable; and therefore nothing could be done except to speak to poor No. 19 on the vanity of human hopes in general, and more especially of such as were founded on the possibility of righteous dealing by a man who had already cruelly wronged her. As may be supposed, these vague sentiments had little weight with the high–spirited, impassioned woman. She thought only of the long period of dreary imprisonment which she had suffered for this man's sake, and could not, would not doubt that he had a great recompense in store for her. At length the day of her release came—so long looked forward to as the golden dawn of a life that would be like a summer day in brightest happiness. The visitor went to take the poor woman from the prison, and place her in safety in the home provided for her. Once outside the gates of the jail, she was of course entirely exempt from prison rule, and the truth could be told to her without any breach of duty,—a sufficiently painful task! but delay was for every reason undesirable, and it had to be done at once. The fact of her lover's recent marriage was disclosed. There was silence for a moment. At last, with a wild fierceness in her eyes like that of a hunted animal driven to bay, she muttered hoarsely, "He promised to marry me," and then closed her lips resolutely over the tempest of indignation that raged within her. After that all went wrong with her. She became embittered and hopeless. She seemed to have lost faith in human nature, and with it went also the first faint stirrings of belief in a Love Divine which had been evoked in her during her prison experience. She was speedily again in communication with the outer world, and temptation came from various quarters to draw her back into the vortex of London life. She was found one day surrounded by a quantity of new music which had been sent to her, and letters followed respecting property said to have been bequeathed to her for which her presence was required. Within a fortnight of her discharge from jail she had drifted back into London, nominally only for a little time, but in fact to disappear altogether from the know– ledge of those who had taken so much interest in her, with ominous indications that she was likely to take a downward path. There remained only the hope that in the dark days which were certain to overtake her in her perilous career, the remembrance of noble aims and pure desires which had been aroused within her while a prisoner, might yet return to bless and brighten her later years of life.

The restrictions surrounding a prison visitor which are illustrated by this history are, however, as nothing in comparison to the one great difficulty which in many different shapes presents itself to all who have to work among the inmates of a jail. This simply consists in the complete reversal of all preconceived ideas as to the clearly defined limits of right and wrong, when these are brought into connection with a certain impracticable class of prisoners.

To such as they are and have been from in fancy, it seems impossible to apply any laws, human or divine. They have been a law unto themselves all their days, as their parents were before them, and have literally known no other. Absolutely ignorant of so much as the existence of any Power which could enforce a moral obligation,—the name of God never heard by them except in the form of an oath,—the enactments of the Legislature are only recognised as that which must be deftly cheated and defied with all possible cunning. For instance, how could guilt in the ordinary sense of the word be held to attach to a young woman who breaks the commandment "Thou shalt not steal," when not only she never heard of the prohibition, nor of the Being from whom it emanated, but, on the contrary, had been taught from childhood that nothing could be so righteous and so clever as to accomplish a successful theft, and bring the proceeds home to receive a just reward—while the extreme iniquity of failing in a clumsy attempt at the noble art would be rightly visited by the heaviest punishment? In giving this illustration we are drawing no fancy picture. Persons answering to that description are frequently received in our penal establishments; but we will give the details of one typical case, which certainly sounds strangely enough, as the record of a true existence in the midst of our boasted civilisation and enlightenment.

A women was transferred to our prison from one of the overflowing convict institutions, under a long sentence. She was aged thirty–four years, and, as usual, the list of her previous convictions was sent in along with her. From this official document we learned that she had already been imprisoned sixty–four times. It was a curious coincidence that the number of her terms of incarceration almost exactly doubled her years of life, but such was undoubtedly the fact. She looked even younger than her actual age. She was a small, dark–eyed woman, whose countenance when she was brought into the jail bore a somewhat evil expression; it was at least characterised by abiding sullenness and ill–temper, and at first her conduct seemed to correspond with it. She was refractory so far as she dared, and gave a good deal of trouble to the officers set over her; but after a time of intercourse with her unofficial visitor, she became a totally changed being—gentle, obedi– ent, and deeply grateful to those whom she found, to her utter amazement, were really anxious to help and comfort her. Never before, in all the years of her miserable life, had this poor forlorn outcast known what it was to meet with pity or kindness from her fellow–creatures, and the first touch of human sympathy fell on the hard defiance of her despairing darkened spirit like a ray of warm sunshine on ice that binds imprisoned waters. Very soon she yielded to the yearning that, as we have said, arises in hours of solitary confinement, to pour out to some friendly listener the mournful secrets of the past: and the whole black record of a most hopeless existence was revealed in her own simple uncouth language.

"I never had no home," she began, "no, nor yet a friend—never, never. I've been full of trouble and misery all my days, and there was never any one—man or woman, rich or poor—to hold out a hand to me, and help me struggle out of it. They wouldn't even let me alone, but they used to knock me about and force me to thieve and fight for them, and then they made off and left me to be caught by the police and locked up. The first kind words as any one ever spoke to me have been in this here prison." Then she went on and told all her history, which we retail in fewer words. It was true to the letter that she had never had a home. Her father had been a street musician, and her mother spent all her time wandering from place to place hawking anything she could find to sell. "Hawking" in that class is very well known to be a scarcely concealed pretence for begging or stealing whenever the opportunity presents itself. At night the family retired to any one of the low lodging–houses in the East End of London which had room for them; and when the few necessary pence failed for even that uninviting shelter, they slept in a railway arch or under some empty truck in a siding where they escaped notice. Never, in her earlier years, did hapless No. 12 know what it was to lay her head in any more decent sleeping–place than the common room of one of those terrible dens, where men and women of the most degraded class are herded together. Even such semblance of care and protection as a father and mother so circumstanced could give her, was not long retained by the unfortunate girl. Her father was an inveterate drunkard: he started on his street round one day in his usual health, and before night fell he was found dead from suffocation after a drinking–fit, in which some ill–bestowed shilling had enabled him to indulge. His wife, if such she was, did not protract the period of mourning for him. Very speedily she annexed another protector; and she seems after that to have abandoned all care for her child, so that it made very little difference to No. 12 when the close of her mother's career came as suddenly as that of her father. After a cold winter's night, when the woman and her so–called husband had not the means of paying even for leave to sit up in the lodging–house kitchen, which is sometimes granted to those who cannot afford a bed, she was discovered lying across his feet stone dead from exposure in the street. Thenceforward there existed no one on earth from whom No. 12 could claim support or protection. Her first imprison– ment took place at the age of ten years—the punishment of a theft from a shop, not by any means her earliest. The result of this sentence was, however, to give her the best chance of rescue from evil that her sad destiny had ever afforded her. She was sent to a reformatory. It must to some extent have been an advantage to her, as she there learned to read, though imperfectly enough. It does not seem, however, as if any effective moral influence had been brought to bear upon her, for it is certain that she came out from that *quasi* prison, after a not very long detention, with her ideas of right and wrong as entirely distorted as they had always been. She was placed by the managers of the institution in a farmhouse to act as "general servant" (slavey, she would have termed it) to the farmer's wife. Her tenure of this respectable employment came quickly to an abrupt conclusion. She had been sent out one fine day into the fields, and being struck with surprise and enthusiasm at the sight of wild flowers actually growing, so unlike the faded nose–gays she had seen in the London streets, she remained there gathering them long past the time when she had been ordered by her mistress to return. It was probably the first innocent employment on which she had ever voluntarily been engaged, and the farmer's wife punished her for it by instant dismissal. No. 12 was sent back alone into the London streets with the very few shillings in her pocket which constituted the wages she had earned. With these she proudly engaged a room for herself, child as she still was; and having made a passing acquaintance with a woman who lived opposite, she inquired of her whether she knew of any situation vacant for a "slavey." After various tentative experiences she drifted into a house of very bad character. Happily a stand–up fight with one of the inmates caused her to be ignominiously cast out of it, and from thence she went to serve in a public–house.

That was the end of all dim efforts at honest living. She was by that time about sixteen years of age, and she very speedily took the last fatal step in ruin and degradation, not even prompted thereto by any personal affection. No one tried to protect or save her; no one told her that there were sin and misery in a shameless life on the streets, and to that she passed hardly knowing what she did. In that terrible existence she remained. It was varied only by perpetual imprisonments, sometimes for assault—she had a fierce temper, which she never dreamt of controlling; very often for theft; occasionally for breaking the plate–glass windows of a gin–palace. So she went on from one condition of wretchedness to another, tossed like a hapless piece of driftwood on the waves of this troublesome world;—beaten, bruised in body and mind; ill–treated, knocked down by drunken men;—dragged, resisting and half–intoxicated, to prison by the police,—feeling that every one with whom she came in contact was her enemy; suffering continual pain and privation, from which she knew no way of escape, save by that which better–instructed persons held to be error and wickedness. Worn with the struggle against her bitter fate, at length she found herself flung inside the walls of our prison. It certainly seemed as if hers was as desperate a case for the possibility of moral improvement as had ever come under the notice of chaplain or visitor, yet they could not feel that it was by any means hopeless. It was perfectly evident that after she left the reformatory this poor woman never had the ghost of a chance, in all her trampled–down existence, of rising to higher and purer hopes than those involved in the passion of the moment, or of learning any other distinction between right and wrong than that which brought greater or less misery to herself. The extraordinary change which took place in her demeanour and conduct when she realised that she was indeed no longer to be left friendless and unpitied, justified the hopes which were soon entertained that she would do well in the new position of honest and honourable living which was prepared for her acceptance on her discharge from jail. It remains to be seen whether these hopes will be realised in the future.

We cannot close this chapter with so sad a history, and must be allowed to relieve the gloom of our preceding pages by a brief account of one of the strangest, as well as the most comical, little personages who ever came under the grave, quiet authority of the prison warders, and whose case was, above all others, difficult to deal with, so far as the moral law was concerned. She was a diminutive elderly woman, with a countenance full of vivacity and cleverness, and the keenest of black eyes, which sparkled with malicious amusement whenever she succeeded in perplexing the officers by some odd proceeding. She had a certain air of refinement piercing through even the coarse convict garb, and was undoubtedly a person of considerable education. She was always extremely cheerful, and talked volubly and freely with the prison visitor, who alone was allowed to converse privately with her. It was plain that she had known society of a very different grade from most of her fellow–prisoners, and it might even have been inferred from her manner that she had been in some capacity at Court, or at least had managed to become acquainted with the traditions of that exclusive sphere, for she would insist, most inappropriately, on treating her visitor to royal honours. Never did she approach that individual without making three profound curtsies at different stages of the advance, and invariably retired backward from the august presence with the same elaborate ceremony. Apparently she had travelled much; and on one occasion when she was getting the worst of an ethical argument with her visitor, and she was desirous of changing the subject of conversation, she burst into a torrent of French on a totally different theme, and spoke it faultlessly with an admirable Parisian accent.

Who she was, whence she came, and whither she went, when, refusing almost all help in the most independent manner, she disappeared outside the prison gates on her discharge, could never be elicited from her by any means whatever. She was, however, open as the day respecting the offence which had brought her within the grasp of the law. She described it minutely—first emphasising the fact that she considered it a most proper and virtuous proceeding. She had broken into a house, she said, when the family were at church, and had taken therefrom some valuable property, with which she was comfortably departing when, unfortunately, a contemptible spy had not only watched her clever proceedings, but was actually base enough to give information to the police. The cool self–satisfaction with which she related this daring theft is quite indescribable.

As it was the duty of the prison visitor to try and bring her to a better mind, some allusion was naturally made to the Eighth Commandment; upon which she said, with a slightly supercilious smile, that she was perfectly cognisant of that injudicious enactment, and entirely disapproved of it. It was, she affirmed, illogical, improper, unjust, and no sensible person would pay the smallest attention to it. She then proceeded to prove the moral obligation she had been under to commit this burglary. Her mode of reasoning showed that she must have been consorting with Socialists and Communists, probably in France as well as in England.

"The matter is perfectly simple," she said; "those people whose house I entered—through the window —and from whom I **took** (stealing is a very vulgar word) some trumpery articles, were extremely wealthy; they had everything they could desire in the world, and more a great deal than they required, while I had nothing—not even on that particular day the means of providing myself with comfortable meals: it was perfectly right and proper, therefore, that I should avail myself of their superfluity. Why should they have more than they needed and I nothing? It would have been more suitable, indeed, if I could have remained long enough to make a just division of the whole property between myself and them; my only blunder was in not being a little more sharp and careful, so as to evade those infamous policemen, who will occupy themselves pertinaciously with the affairs of other people."

When the old woman arrived at this point in her discourse, an attempt was made by her listener to take a somewhat different view of the transaction, but it was only received by her with a patronising smile and a wave of the hand, with which she dismissed the argument.

"Yes," she said, "I perceive that these are your principles, and no doubt they are shared by a few persons who hold to the old traditions; but I have been assured by those who have the interests of the people really at heart that they are obsolete, quite obsolete. There is a good time coming when there will be a very different distribution of property, and the right adjustment of the matter will not be only in this world,"—then she nodded her head significantly, and hinted that so well–informed a person as the visitor must doubtless be quite aware of the probable unpleasant destination of the rich in a future state.

This provoking old personage was certainly a most peculiar specimen of a prisoner. She took all the pains and penalties of her position, even the uninviting diet which is usually much deplored, in the most airy and cheerful manner imaginable. She effectually baffled any attempt at the improvement of her mind and morals. Some steps were taken at the time of her release to give her facilities for gaining an honest living, but there was not much reason to hope that she would really avail herself of them. It was evident that she intended to continue her system of profiting by other people's superfluities; and as she was far advanced in life, it seemed probable that she would end her days during some long term of penal servitude.

We need scarcely say that the few instances we have now given do not represent the gravest perplexities with which the appointed visitor to a prison has to contend: there are others much more serious, as well as more sorrowful, on which we have not yet touched. But whatever may be the difficulties of the work, we must repeat our conviction that the employment of efficient voluntary workers is the only means whereby our prisons could—in addition to their present use as mere places of punishment—become also active agencies for the amelioration of the criminal classes. The police–court missions and prisoners' aid societies, which are established in most large towns, deserve all credit for the amount of good work they succeed in accomplishing; but they can only reach the criminal after his release, when the first breath of recovered freedom acts like a sort of intoxication on his senses, and renders him too often impervious to all but the wild desire to rush away into the old lawless life, with the boon companions who are generally waiting at the prison gate to welcome him back to their ranks. These agencies meet him at a great disadvantage; but it is very different when he is under the sobering influence of a long imprisonment, when the advice and instruction given to him are matured by reflection in the solitude of his cell, and when definite arrangements can be made beforehand for starting him on a better way of life immediately on his discharge. We have been the more anxious to ventilate this question of prison reform because there seems reason to hope, as we have said, that the necessity for an organisation of free volunteer workers is making itself felt at headquarters, and that the dread naturally existing in the minds of the jail authorities respecting so great an innovation of established rule, may gradually be overcome by a clearer comprehension of the great interests involved in the question.

CHAPTER IV. THE DESIRE OF DEATH.

"A little struggle at first, of course,
A little gasping for one more breath,
A little agony, nothing worse,
And then the long sweet sleep of death."**THE** many singular phases of human life with
which the visitor to a prison is naturally made acquainted, do not constitute by any means
the strangest spectacle to be witnessed within those silent walls. A much more
remarkable phenomenon may be studied there, in the peculiar aspect which death
assumes in that region of sin and sorrow and remorse. In the outside world, as we all
know only too well, not even the brightness of immortal hopes can altogether dispel the
gloom and sadness which surround that inexorable mystery. Should the tyranny of life
strip it of all terrors for ourselves, still nothing can assuage the anguish of surrendering
the objects of our helpless love to its stern demand; and habituated as we thus are, to see
it ever hanging like a menacing shadow over the fairest joys existence has to offer us, it
strikes on the consciousness with a weird sense of wonder and awe to meet it in the
attractive guise it wears within the prisoner's cell. Not for themselves, or for any whom
they love, do these erring way–worn men and women dread the last mysterious change;
its poetical name—the "angel of death"—is to them a blest reality. It has for them no
gloom, no repulsion; it is their hope, their desire—always their best, often their only
friend. What must life have been to them when the thought of escape from it is so dear
and sweet that death is most eagerly sought, and ever welcome! They look forward to it
as the gracious termination of the long–borne pain of existence—the cessation of
consciousness, which in their experience is mainly suffering—the triumphant release
from bonds and punishment and the iron power of the law, against which, living, they
must ever struggle in vain. It must not be supposed, however, that they are influenced in
this respect by the vague impression that their last hour on earth may possibly usher them
into a brighter and more–enduring existence,—it is the mere fact of death in its freedom
and rest, wholly unconnected with any idea of a future state, which shines like a star of
hope before their eager eyes. Seldom indeed does it occur to them to look in any sense
beyond it. "To die, to sleep,"—thus far they go with Hamlet; but they never follow him to
the deeper issue—"In that sleep of death, what dreams may come!" If the teaching and

efforts of others force upon their knowledge some possibility of a conscious life beyond the grave which lures them with its untroubled rest, the visions thus evoked are all too dim and shadowy to carry their gaze past that reality of death itself which seems to them so blissful. They know its outward aspect,—they have beheld it often; they have seen a fellow—prisoner carried out from those impregnable walls, "free among the dead"; they have looked on the once tormented, storm—tossed frame sunk in profound repose—eyes that were wont to weep scalding tears, closed in tranquil slumber—hands that toiled in vain to win the bread which at last they snatched by crime, folded in calm inaction on the quiet breast. This is enough; it is real, it is tangible; and to that haven of peace, when the fever and struggle of life are over, they look with inexpressible desire, that often cannot wait the legitimate hour for its gratification.

Certain true histories which have come within the range of our experience will sufficiently show that we are not trusting to any vague theories, in thus describing the beneficent and alluring aspect which death wears within the Silent World, and these are not by any means confined to cases of actual suicide. The passionate belief in the last dread change, as the greatest boon life can offer, has been seen by us to take action in forms much more singular than mere self—destruction. One of the strangest instances of a man enamoured of death that ever came under our notice was that of an old agricultural labourer, whom we will call Richard Hodson. He was about sixty years of age, absolutely illiterate, of sound mind so far as his intelligence went, but without an idea beyond his daily work and the circumstances of his domestic life. He had apparently no religious belief. If any dim recollections remained with him of the Sunday—school teaching of his childish days, it never seemed to occur to him that they could have any personal reference to his own destiny here or hereafter. There was a church in his native village, but he never entered it; and the only mode of "saying his prayers," of which his wife sometimes spoke, was simply by his use of language more undesirably forcible than usual. Hodson's life had been singularly devoid of any element of pleasure or happiness. It had been spent in ceaseless grinding toil to procure the bare means of subsistence, and the home to which he returned after his day's labour was rendered distasteful to him by the sullen temperament of his wife, his only companion. He had but one child—a daughter—and she lived at a dis— tance, entirely separated from him by her marriage with a man who had treated her wrongly, and with whom, therefore, Hodson had a deadly quarrel. It would have been hard to say whether he or his wife was the most thoroughly ill—tempered. They often passed days and even weeks together in their small cottage without addressing a single syllable to each other. It was not a cheerful abode under the circumstances; and certainly Richard Hodson's existence was altogether so hopelessly unattractive, that he might be forgiven for not caring particularly to prolong it.

One beautiful evening in the month of May the man came home after having been hard at work from early daylight. There was a small kitchen–garden attached to his cottage, on which he and his wife depended entirely for a supply of vegetables with which to eke out their scanty meals. Some piece of work within its narrow limits required to be finished at once, if they were not to lose the benefit of the uncertain fine weather; but the man was tired, and he felt that he must have efficient help if he was to get the necessary task done that night. He asked his wife if she would go with him to the garden and give him her assistance for an hour, so that they might provide against the chance of rain on the morrow. She answered that she would see him far enough before she lifted a finger to help him in that or in anything else. Thereafter a fit of desperation seemed to take possession of the man. A frantic desire seized him to make an end of the weary intolerable business of existence altogether, both for himself and the woman who so ingeniously managed to intensify its bitterness. He felt that if he obeyed this strong impulse without delay, the proceeding would have the additional advantage of enabling him to taste the sweets of revenge, which at that moment appeared to him peculiarly delectable; and, in short, the whole transaction assumed so bewitching an aspect to his mind, that he did not hesitate in accomplishing it fully then and there. Within an hour from the time when his wife refused to work with him in their little garden, he had most effectually made an end of her, and was himself in the safe custody of the police on his way to the county jail. He surrendered himself to them with the utmost cheerfulness when they approached with the handcuffs, and made but this one remark—"Now I'll go to the gallows like a prince."

These words, or others to the same effect, he repeated at intervals during the few weeks which elapsed before he took his trial; and there can be no question that they embodied the feeling which was uppermost in his mind.

Hodson could neither read nor write, and the time hung somewhat heavy on his hands, while waiting till his fate should be settled at the Assizes. He therefore welcomed the present writer eagerly to his cell, as the visit afforded him an opportunity for a little conversation; but it was all on one theme—how ready and anxious he was to die. Nothing could be said to give him the least idea that his wish in this respect would not be ratified. The cruel deed he had so strangely committed seemed to have been completely motiveless and inexcusable, and it was plain that no available steps could be taken by any one to avert the consequences. In fact, when the day of his trial arrived, the man's absolute determination to die frustrated the humane and anxious efforts of his judge to give him any chance of escape that might be justified by the law. Nothing could exceed the kindness and consideration shown by Sir — to this unhappy criminal, in marked contrast to what occurred with regard to a case we have already had an opportunity of describing in these pages. Had there been the slightest possible ground on which his crime could have been reduced to manslaughter, the high–minded judge would gladly have availed himself of it; but Richard Hodson rendered any idea of the kind abortive, by insisting, in defiance of all the advice given him, on pleading guilty to wilful murder.

It is extremely rare in the annals of our courts of justice that such a plea should be recorded—not more than once, we believe, in a century; and of course, if accepted, it could only, according to the existing law, be followed by an immediate sentence of death.

The man's words, firm and decided, "I am guilty," were heard with dismay by all in the court; but the judge was resolved, if possible, not to allow his self–condemnation to be received as final, and the conversation which ensued between him and the prisoner was so singular, that we give it verbatim as it was taken down by the shorthand writer at the time, omitting only some irrelevant remarks.

"Before I accept that plea," said the judge, "I wish you thoroughly to understand that you are charged with wilful murder–that is to say, causing the death of your wife, meaning to murder her. If that is what you mean to say, you plead guilty to an offence for which you will be sentenced to be changed by the neck till you be dead, within a fortnight of the present time. Do you mean that you desire to plead guilty to that, and undergo the consequences—do you mean that?"

" I done the deed, sir; I killed her dead."

"That is not murder," replied the judge, "The offence you are charged with, is that of killing her intending to kill her dead. That is murder; the other would be manslaughter. Do you wish to plead guilty to the offence of murder, for which you will have to be hanged in about a fortnight, or do you wish to be tried? Prisoner, do you wish to be tried, or do you wish to be hanged? "

Scenes from a Silent World

"I wish to be hanged, sir—out of it—yes!"

"Whether you are guilty or not?" asked the judge.

"I am guilty, sir."

"I think it a little doubtful whether you really do understand the law which is applicable in this case—and if there is any doubt, it is better that the offence should be investigated by a jury, so that the exact truth may be known"

"I have nothing more to say," said the prisoner; "I done the deed, and must put up with the consequences."

Some discussion ensued between the judge, the counsel, and others as to whether the man understood the difference between murder and man–slaughter.

The judge then again addressed the prisoner: "I think this is really a case in which one ought to have the matter investigated. I must enter a plea of not guilty, that you may be tried." The necessary formality was gone through, and then the judge continued: "You will have to be tried, because I have entered a plea of not guilty. Do you wish to conduct you own case, or would you like some Counsel to appear for you and make the best case he can for you?"

"I would sooner have it now, and done with it," answered the prisoner. "I don't want anybody to plead anything for me, sir—nothing at all."

"You do not wish me to assign Counsel for you?"

"No, sir."

"As you are going to be tried, I offer that there should be some Counsel to see that you have fair–play—do you wish that?"

"I would sooner have it settled, and done away with—over and done with."

"It cannot be settled now," replied the judge; "you will have to be tried to—morrow: all I ask is, whether on your trial you wish to conduct your own case, or whether you would like some Counsel to speak for you?"

"I don't want anybody to talk for me—I will take it in my own hands."

There was nothing more to be said, and the prisoner was removed, but the judge did not desist from his efforts to induce the man to allow a Counsel to be assigned to him next day, and finally this was done. Hodson was fairly driven into giving a most unwilling consent. The Counsel did his best: he made a very eloquent speech, in which he attempted to set up a plea of insanity, but, as might have been expected, it failed completely. Not only did all the persons called to give evidence bear witness to the prisoner's previous soundness of mind, but it was impossible for any one to look at the quiet self—controlled man, who listened with imperturbable composure to the history of his own deed of violence, without feeling satisfied that he was in perfect possession of his faculties and reason. The trial ended with the inevitable result, and Richard Hodson heard his sentence of death with as calm and cheerful a countenance as if it had been the announcement of some rare piece of good fortune. He maintained the same unmoved contented demeanour during the interval which elapsed between his trial and execution. He was very willing to listen to the chaplain's instructions, if only *pour passer le temps*; and it seemed quite an agreeable surprise to him to discover that when he had got rid of this extremely unsatisfactory existence, it was possible that a different form of life, somewhat better and happier, might then open out before him. He was quite docile in accomplishing all that he was told to do in the way of religious preparation with a view to that contingency, but it is doubtful whether the pleasant certainty that he was about "to be hanged, and out of it—yes!" did not loom so large in his mind as the sum of his desires, that little space was left for any less tangible hope. Yet there were various indications that this strange complacency, in prospect of a dreadful doom, was not the mere brutish indifference of a low order of intelligence. Hodson showed feeling in many ways, as well as a strong sense of gratitude, tinctured with astonishment, for the sympathy and kindness manifested towards him in the jail. This was shown in a touching little incident on the Sunday before his death. The chaplain was wont, on these sad occasions, to let the condemned man choose the hymns himself for the last service in which he would join with his fellow—prisoners, and naturally those selected were always such as were suitable to the dying.

Scenes from a Silent World

It is one of the experiences of a prison visitor, which is certainly not enviable, to have to meet the wistful gaze of a man standing up, strong and healthful in full vigour of life, while he sings such words as these, "Hold Thou Thy cross before my closing eyes," knowing that his own undimmed eyes would be closed in death within a few hours. Under these circumstances, during the last service which Richard Hodson attended, the writer, who was accompanying the hymn on the harmonium, involuntarily looked up at him, and was surprised to see him suddenly turn his head away and burst into tears. He had always been so cheerful, that it could only be supposed the full horror of his position had suddenly revealed itself to him; and under that impression the chaplain, on being told after service of the man's unusual agitation, went at once to his cell to offer such consolation as might be possible. He found, however, to his surprise, that the condemned criminal's emotion had not been in the least on his own account. He had observed, he said, that when the visitor glanced at him during the singing of the mournful hymn, it had been with a look of pain and distress; and the idea that he had thus caused a person wholly unconnected with his crime to suffer grief for his sake, as well as several others who were, he knew, greatly troubled at his fate, had shown him that a man's evil deeds go far beyond himself in their malevolent influence, and he felt suddenly overcome with a sort of remorse—it had gone to his heart, he said, and forced from his eyes the tears he would not have shed for himself.

Hodson's indomitable cheerfulness on the fateful morning was such as the prison officials had never before witnessed in any case. He was to die at eight o'clock. At seven he went through a private religious service in the chapel. At half–past seven his breakfast was brought to him in his cell: he drew a chair to the table and sat down to it with an excellent appetite; he proceeded to go through all the little processes necessary for making the best of the food set before him, in the most leisurely manner possible. He was still engaged upon it when the ominous knock came to the door which announced the executioner; then he quietly laid down the last mouthful of bread he had been about to eat, and yielded himself up to the hands that in five minutes more had finished their work upon him.

It seems right, in the interests of other criminals who may have to meet the same doom, to state what occurred at the execution of Richard Hodson, though we will touch on the painful facts as briefly as we can. The unfortunate man suffered a death to which he had not been condemned by law—he was, in fact, violently decapitated. In the opinion of the bystanders, this frightful catastrophe occurred entirely through the mismanagement of the official most concerned. The manner in which that individual treated the matter at the inquest, was not calculated to allay the universal indignation aroused by the event: he spoke of it with careless unconcern, as a little accident which was quite likely to happen often on these occasions, and which simply could not be helped. This opinion was endorsed, only in more gentlemanly terms, by an answer given to a question asked in Parliament respecting the case of Hodson. It was then again affirmed that such occurrences might be expected when the physical characteristics of the criminals were of a nature to produce them.

If there must be a death penalty in England, it would surely be well that it should be accomplished in such a way as to render similar cruelties impossible. Since the first day of the present year, it has been the law in America that executions should be carried out by electricity. Whether or not this may be a desirable mode of operation, it would at all events prevent such terrible occurrences as that which took place at the death of Richard Hodson.

Persons comforted themselves on that occasion, as they are wont to do under other aspects of the final mystery, by the assumption that at least death had been instantaneous. This is not a subject which ought to be discussed in these pages, but we cannot leave it without the simple statement, founded on recent experiments in France and elsewhere which have conclusively proved the fact,—that it is not possible to assign to any fixed time the cessation of consciousness. So far as the investigation has gone at present, there is ample evidence that it endures to a later period after the breath ceases, than has been supposed to be the case hitherto.

The ethics of suicide, as they may be studied within the Silent World, offer many problems for serious consideration. It is an indictable offence, and we have therefore the opportunity of seeing it under very varied aspects, some of which we shall exemplify by giving an account of a few typical cases. In one respect, however, they are all absolutely identical, and that is in the immutable conviction, on the part of the persons concerned, that they have a perfect right to destroy their own lives if it pleases them to do so, and that the act does not render them guilty of any sin in the sight of God, although it has been decreed that it should be reckoned an infringement of human laws. So far as the experience of the present writer extends, it has been found completely impossible to convince men and women who are desirous of ridding themselves of the burden of existence, that they will commit even a venial error by accomplishing their own release. It is simply useless, in discussing the question with them, to call it the crime of self–murder, or to talk of the sanctity of human life which God alone can give, and therefore He alone has a right to recall. Nothing can shake their immovable conviction that their life is given them as a prey to make of it what they will. In the case of prisoners who are suffering punishment for the attempt to put an end to their existence, there is sometimes a diplomatic endeavour, from mere policy, to give an assent to the moral reflections pressed upon them; but when driven to speak their minds honestly, they invariably repeat that they see no reason why they should not get quit as they please of an embarrassing possession, with which no one but themselves has any concern whatever.

This mode of dealing with the subject is per– haps natural enough on the part of persons who have never taken any serious view of their moral responsibilities, but it is less easy to account for the extraordinary light–heartedness with which, for the most part, they are ready to plunge into the unknown darkness of the last mysterious change. As we have already said, no thought of what may lie beyond disturbs their mind; but it might have been imagined that the ghastly associations of the grave, and its slow decay, would at least have moved them to some shrinking from the physical results of dissolution. It is not so: they take the fatal step as easily and carelessly as they would lay themselves down to sleep in their bed.

"If you had succeeded in your attempt to kill yourself," the writer said to a young prisoner who had been rescued almost lifeless from the river where she had flung herself, "you would have been lying now cold and stiff under the coffin–lid, unable to see the light of day or to hear the voice of a friend, and with no time left for repentance, or even so much as a prayer to the God whose commandment you were breaking. Are you not thankful to be restored to life and the opportunity of amendment?"

"No," she said, lightly; "for if they had let me alone, I should have been done with it all, and had no more trouble or worry, and that was just what I wanted. I wish they had left me at the bottom of the river."

Sometimes the immediate causes which lead to suicide seem strangely disproportioned to the gravity of the step. One girl, who was ready to fling maledictions at her rescuers, had three several times done her best to put an end to her existence. On two of these occasions she had, so far as her own will was concerned, practically succeeded—once by poison, and once by strangulation. She was to all appearance dead, after one desperate attempt, and would very soon have been so in reality, but for the care and toil bestowed on her by a kindly physician who was sent for on the discovery of her condition, and who spent a whole night in unceasing efforts to restore animation. He succeeded at last, and she did not thank him! She was given up to what she and her companions of the same unhappy class term with unconscious irony "a gay life," and she did find a fitful hollow enjoyment in the excitement of evenings spent in theatres and dancing–booths, and in the extravagant dresses and jewellery with which she adorned herself; but there came to her sudden moments, when the whole brilliant phantasmagoria of her existence would seem to roll away from her, and the reality of her position appear in its true colours, and straightway, without an instant's hesitation, she would take the best means in her power to divest herself of it altogether. She exemplified the truism that extremes meet. For the manner in which the subject is regarded by these, the lowest outcasts of the people, is exactly similar to the view taken of it by the high–class leaders of society in modern France, where it is the fashion now to say, "On vit parceque à moins de se tuer—on ne peut pas faire autrement." The hapless inmates of our prisons, however, consider the alternative of killing themselves preferable to an unwilling endurance of the primary evil.

While the recklessness and indifference with which suicide is resorted to is almost universal in the lower stratum of society, the causes which lead to the impulse are of course very varied, and often most pathetic. A poor old woman, who had nearly reached the Scriptural threescore years and ten, was sentenced lately to a short term of imprisonment for attempting self–destruction. It had very nearly been successful, and in fact was so in the end, as the shock to her system from immersion in ice–cold water proved fatal, and she only lived one week after her release from jail. She related her simple history with the utmost composure. She had lived happily and respectably with her husband from the time of her early marriage in youth. He had a pension as a retired soldier, which supported them in comparative comfort when he was too old to work. Their home for twenty–eight years had been the little cottage in which he died at the commencement of an unusually severe winter. "He had been an angel," the poor woman said—"so good and steady, and so kind to her;" and when he was gone, she clung with passionate attachment to the little house in which she had spent so many happy years with him—but she could not pay the rent. His pension had of course expired with him, and she was, in fact, without the means of living at all. She began by selling her little possessions one after another in order to obtain food, and in this way she managed to live for a few weeks. When everything was gone except the scanty furniture of one room, the landlord appeared and claimed it for his unpaid rent. It was all carted away, including even the chest containing her clothing: then he turned her into the street and locked the door. There was but one refuge open to her on earth—the work–house; but that last abode of wretchedness seems to hold a place in the minds of the poor—undeservedly we think—equivalent in horror to one of the circles of Dante's Inferno. The idea of going to the "Union," as she would have called it, does not seem to have occurred to the forlorn widow. She looked back for a moment at the closed door of her little earthly paradise, and then took her way shivering through a public park to the river. There, without apparently the slightest shrinking or dread, she flung herself into the water under a cold wintry sky. Two men happened to be going past in a boat. They rescued her just as she was sinking; and after consciousness had been restored, she was brought to the prison. She passed the time of her sojourn there in a strange dreamy state, talking only of her husband, and her hope of seeing him perhaps again if she could succeed in "getting out of this weary world." The hope of reunion had successfully been suggested to her mind by the religious consolations afforded to her in the prison, but it proved completely impossible to persuade her that she had not been perfectly justified in trying to die. She would have been quite willing to have repeated the experiment the moment she was free to do so, if death had not mercifully come to her uncalled, and thus at last her desire was granted.

A young man was once committed to jail on the same charge, who had acted apparently with as little thought of all that death might mean, as had been manifested by the simple old widow; but his case was otherwise in marked contrast to hers.

He had been fairly well educated, the son of a respectable tradesman who lived with his family in London, and the young man was extremely pleasing both in appearance and manners. It happened that the writer saw him for the first time when he was being conveyed to the jail by the police, immediately after he had been taken out of the river in which he had tried to drown himself. It was rather a piteous spectacle: his hat had been lost, and his fair hair, dripping wet, hung over his eyes, that were glancing vaguely from side to side. He walked feebly, leaning heavily on his grim supporters, and had altogether a bewildered look, as if he could not understand how he happened to be still alive. Under the circumstances the visitor was very glad to be left alone with him in the prison cell next day, in order to hear from him what had led to his abhorrence of life at an age when it is wont to wear its brightest hues before the unclouded eyes of youth. He was quite willing to tell his story without reserve; but the sum and substance of his explanation was simply this: "I could not face my mother."

Scenes from a Silent World

He had been expected home for a holiday on the evening of the day when he had flung his young life to the river depths. He had preferred to lie "uncoffined and unannealed" rather than meet his mother's reproachful eyes. He had been the best loved of her children—apparently, as is often the case, just because he had been the wildest and most unmanageable. His brothers and sisters were all doing well in good situations—steady and respectable—helping their parents out of their earnings; but he had never been successful in anything, simply because his roving disposition had led him to abandon every employment he had tried, after a short time, and go off in quest of something new. He had been unstable and thoughtless, fond of amusement, and, above all, of his liberty; but he did not seem to have been addicted to vice of any kind. A spendthrift, however, he had been most emphatically, and his mother had again and again struggled to pay his debts and give him a fresh start in some new career. This she had done a very few months previously, and a good opening had been found for him in a provincial city. She had furnished him with the means of establishing him in it, and had made a heartfelt appeal to him to give up his careless, unsatisfactory ways, and set himself to work hard for his living in an honest, respectable manner. She told him that if he failed again, she did not think it would be possible for her to help him out of any further difficulty. She had come to an end of her resources, and this was really his last chance and hers; if he again came back to her penniless and in debt, it would break her heart. Thus far the young man had gone quickly through his history, but when he came to that point he turned his head away, shamefaced and crimson to the temples, with tears in his eyes. Then he owned that the love of pleasure and freedom had again been too much for him. The weather had been beautiful and sunny; the duties of his post kept him at grinding toil amid dust and gloom. Without a thought of the future, or of the consequences one way or another, he had broken away from it all, following the first shining temptation that had lured him out to a summer day's enjoyment. Then, ashamed to go back to his employers, yet more ashamed to face his mother, to whom alone he could turn even for food and shelter, he had obeyed a sudden wayward impulse, and flung himself to the embrace of death, with no other thought but that it was a means of escaping his immediate difficulties. It appeared that he had not for a single moment reflected on the dread import of the act, whereby he not only destroyed all the fair promise of a life in this world which had scarce reached maturity, but imperilled also the fairer hopes that might have shone for him in the eternal future.

The term of imprisonment which this young man went through proved to be of incalculable value to him. His advisers within the jail saw that it was a case which required very plain speaking as to the errors of his past, if his future was to be conducted

68

on better principles and more creditable motives. He was not spared any of the stern truths which his unjustifiable conduct demanded; and he had ample time to ponder them in the solitude of his cell. The result was that a really remarkable change took place in him: his eyes were opened to the serious misdeeds of which he had been guilty; and although, in his case as in all others, it was impossible to make him believe that suicide was in itself a crime, he yet did perceive most strongly, how utterly unfit and unprepared he had been for an entrance on the unseen eternity.

When the time came for his release from prison, he found that those who had not hesitated to deal severely with him, so far as his moral turpitude was concerned, were ready to be his true friends in helping him to make a new beginning. Some necessary assistance was given to him; he was reconciled to his parents, and amply fulfilled his promises of amendment. Most satisfactory accounts have been received of him, and of the steadiness and self–denial with which he laboured to support himself in an honest and independent manner. It was one of those cases in which the advantages of the system of prison–workers was strikingly manifest. If this young man had left the jail as reckless and hopeless as when he entered it, the probabilities are that he would at once have taken means to accomplish more effectually than before his final disappearance out of this visible world.

We had another equally successful instance of complete reformation, in the case of a woman, who was, without exception, the most lawless and daring young person whom we ever found trying conclusions with the authority of the prison officials. She was a handsome black–eyed girl, lithe and active, possessed of an inexhaustible fund of energy and vigour, of which she made use in every reckless freak she could think of—not excepting a rush into the realms of death whenever the fancy took her to invade his unseen dominion. The beginning of her troubles in this life had been a stepmother. That especial relation is a fruitful source of evil and misery, to the uncontrolled and undisciplined class which swells the population of our prisons.

No. 14, after a few pitched battles with the functionary who occupied that position in her father's house, had departed one dark night from her home, and was seen of her natural protectors no more. In all the various phases of the wild career on which she entered, she adhered steadfastly to the resolution she had taken that they should never hear of her again, or so much as know whether she were alive or dead. She changed her name, and, delighting in the entire liberty she had achieved, gave all considerations of morals or propriety to the winds, abandoning herself, in fact, to an extremely undesirable mode of existence. She succeeded in committing nearly every offence that could be thought of against the majesty of the law, excepting murder. She was not at all an ill–tempered or covetous woman, and had no animosity against any one, when once safe out of reach of the detested stepmother. Her thefts seemed to be committed rather from a spirit of daring and bravado than from any wish to become possessed of other people's property. Of course she made acquaintance with the interior of a good many prisons. In one of those, situated at some distance from the jail with which the writer is connected, she perpetrated an escapade of a suffi– ciently original nature to be published in the newspapers. She had been summoned to the room of the chief female warder to be reprimanded for some of her customary infractions of rule, and when the officer's back was turned for a moment, she sprang like a cat at the window, shivered the glass, forced herself through the bars, and, at the imminent risk of breaking her neck, dropped from a considerable height to the ground. Just at first she lay stunned; but quickly recovering consciousness, she managed in some unaccountable manner to scale the walls which still intervened between herself and liberty, and the night being pitch–dark, she got clear away before the officers sent in pursuit could succeed in capturing her. She was dressed in the tell–tale convict clothes, and therefore hurried under cover of the darkness to the house of an acquaintance in one of the lowest parts of the town. There, by fair means or foul, she obtained possession of a suit of men's attire, arrayed herself in it, cut off her long hair, and thus disguised, went out into the world in search of fresh adventures. She roamed about at her leisure, having assumed a gruff tone of voice and a swaggering gait, and for a long time no one doubted that she had a right to a place among the lords of the creation; but a misdemeanour of some kind brought her once more into the hands of the police, and then not only was her sex discovered, but her identity also with the prisoner whose daring escape from prison had been heard of in all directions. Finally her career of independence terminated in her being brought under a long sentence to our prison. There unceasing efforts were made to influence the poor girl for good, and to save her from herself,—for she was, in the fullest sense of the word, her own worst enemy; her reckless disposition and untamed passions were the true source of all that she had endured of misery and peril. When the time of her release arrived, she was placed in a safe shelter, and she at once commenced a regular correspondence with the visitor of the jail she had left.

Will it be believed, after the history we have given of her exploits, that when we last received a letter from No. 14, she wrote out of the clois– tered Home of an English Sisterhood,—being herself a professed member of their community, and having, after a

70

severe novitiate, passed to the regular and austere life of a nun, bound by perpetual vows? Yet such is the literal fact; and to those who have had a long experience of the vagaries of human nature in her rank of life, it does not appear so very extraordinary.

No. 14 was really possessed of some very fine qualities underlying her wild impulses, and amongst these was a passionate strength of affection, which had never known any legitimate outlet till she found a friend within the walls of our prison, to whom she attached herself vehemently, and through whom she learnt to know the Supreme Object of an adoration that could alone satisfy and subdue her ardent nature. She had received very little religious teaching of any kind in her young days, but she had always had dim instinctive longings for something better and purer than the life she was leading. When the fair vision was shown to her of a Love that for her sake had been stronger than death, she gave herself up to it with a depth of repentance and a fervour of worship that could not stop short of the utmost limits of self–renunciation. She writes that she has not the smallest desire ever again to leave the silence and monotony of the convent life, and there, it may be concluded, she will remain till her strange career terminates altogether.

Some of the aspects under which death is sought by prisoners for themselves, and even, under certain mournful conditions, for those they love best, are almost too sad to be described in these pages. What, for instance, can be more hopelessly dreary than the idea of a man destroying himself in the absolute solitude and darkness of his prison cell by night? Yet such cases are by no means uncommon. In spite of the sedulous care exercised by the officers to deprive the prisoners of everything which could be used as an instrument of self–destruction, it has been found impossible to prevent the occasional perpetration of the deed. Not long since in the prison of which we write, a man was locked up as usual one evening after cheerfully bidding good–night to the warders in charge. Next morning when his door was opened he was found stone dead, having possessed no other means for accomplishing his purpose than the pocket–handkerchief with which he suspended himself from the gas–pipe, and the extraordinary determination which enabled him to keep his knees bent until he expired. If he had risen to his feet even for a moment, he could not have died.

By many strange expedients is death sought by prisoners, not only for their own release but for that of children too young to seek or desire it. The records of infanticide as they are known within our prisons are very painful, and they would be utterly unaccountable but for the explanation given by Dante, in the celebrated line with which he closes the

account of Ugolino and his sons in the Torre della Fame—
"Poscià piu che il dolor, potè il digiunio." There is a passive form of suicide very frequent among the mysterious race of tramps, which is singular enough to be worthy of a few moments' attention.

The tramps who pervade our country from end to end, and often find their way into jail, are emphatically a most mysterious race, as we have just termed them. They lead a life, by their own indomitable will and determination, which is more hideously miserable than anything which could be imagined. How it can possibly be the voluntary choice of numberless men and women of all ages is simply inexplicable. With the one exception that it is a life of freedom, it seems to lack every element of attraction that could exist for a human being. Their only home is the open highway, along which, summer and winter alike, they tramp aimlessly hour after hour, never knowing from one day to another where they are to lay their head at night. Indeed they often are unable to obtain any shelter at all, and sleep by the roadside or in some open shed, such as was described by a hapless woman in our prison, who found her infant frozen to death in her arms after a night spent in that receptacle. To have begged or stolen a few pence, which enables them to get a bed at a public–house or in some low lodging, is the height of felicity for them; and they consider themselves very unfortunate when bad weather obliges them to take their night's rest in the workhouse, with the understanding that they must pay for it by an hour's hard labour at stone–breaking in the morning; but it is only in the depths of winter that they dream of exposing themselves to so great an inconvenience. In the summer an open field or a dry ditch is thought infinitely preferable.

These tramps have no affinity with the gipsy race, which might perhaps have explained their wandering propensities. They are stolid British men and women, with nothing in the least picturesque or romantic about them. Many of them have been born while their parents were leading this life "on the road," which seems to them so delectable, and the force of habit may to some extent account, in their case, for so strange a mode of existence; but numbers of them deliberately choose it for themselves, often breaking up a settled home, and going off with wife and children to walk miles upon miles every day with their tired swollen feet, not caring apparently what particular place they may happen to reach, only fully decided never again to sleep under a roof of their own.

The more aristocratic members of this roving community provide themselves with a hawker's licence, and, according to their own account, they are enabled to get a sufficient livelihood by the sale of the goods they affect. The women deal largely in nightcaps, which seems to be a favourite article of luxury in country villages; and the men in boot–laces, combs, and tracts of a very fierce and alarming nature. But the truth is, that the hawking business only veils less creditable modes of obtaining money—the most innocent of which is systematic begging; and tramps who pride themselves on not being thieves, will generally admit freely enough that they depend for their subsistence on charity alone. No doubt a love of idleness, as well as of freedom, lies at the root of their adoption of so trying a life; but even with that powerful attraction, it is hard to understand how they can voluntarily endure all the suffering it entails. It might be comprehended if they lived in a southern clime, where frost and snow are unknown, and the peasants dine on a handful of olives with a lump of bread; but in this country, where the winter can bring such terrible forces to bear on their homeless condition, it is marvellous that they should persist in adhering to their life of hardship. The Emperor Nicholas of Russia is said to have trusted to "General January" to rout the British troops in the Crimea, but our tramps do not hesitate to set that power at defiance. Great efforts are made in our prison to find regular employment for them on their release, and so enable them to abandon their vagabond habits, but they invariably refuse to avail themselves of the opportunity.

We had a singular instance of this in the case of a woman eighty–four years of age, who was imprisoned on a short sentence in the late autumn for some slight misdemeanour. When the time for her release came, she prepared deliberately to encounter an English winter on the road, and it seemed evident from her age and infirmity that if she did, she would simply be found dead in a ditch some day from cold and exposure. The strongest efforts were therefore made to induce her to abandon her intention. A home was secured for her in a charitable institution, where she would have had every comfort, and she was told in the plainest terms that she would not live the winter out if she persisted in braving its inclemency. Her only answer was that which we hear again and again from tramps of all ages—"I prefer the road; I mean to go on the road, and do as I have always done." We could not tie the old woman hand and foot, which would have been the only means of preventing her from taking her own way, and so on a cold morning in early winter she passed through the jail gates and disappeared. She has never been heard of since, and it is probable she met the fate predicted for her.

A similar obstinacy was manifested by another lady of mature years, who afforded at the same time a remarkable instance of the mysterious attraction which some persons seem to possess for their fellow–creatures, under the most unfavourable circumstances. She was, without doubt, one of the most hideously ugly women it was possible to see. She had only one eye, and a wooden leg, and her grey hair and wrinkles testified to a very long acquaintance with the vicissitudes of life. Yet she was the beloved of a Frenchman with whom she travelled, and who was supposed, for her sake, to have abandoned his native country and his natural ties. Nothing could induce either the one or the other to separate, though they were in no way legitimately united; or to give up their chosen mode of existence—which consisted in wandering from one public-house to another, where they gained a precarious existence by making most discordant music with their cracked voices, for the amusement of the persons drinking there.

The mystery of the tramp's strange taste for a homeless life is rendered deeper by the fact that it does become, as we have said, a passive form of suicide. It is only the very strongest who can long brave with impunity the constant privation and exposure of their existence,—many of them die quickly from phthisis and bronchitis, or other maladies incidental to their circumstances. When they succumb to a lengthened illness they generally drift into some workhouse, but there are innumerable cases of death by the roadside. Only lately a man was found unconscious near a brick-kiln to which he had crept for warmth, and was taken to a hospital, where he lived for two days, but he was never able to speak. No one knew his name, or anything about him, and his pockets were perfectly empty; so he died an unknown stranger, and was buried in a nameless grave: if he had kith or kin on earth, they can never have known his fate in any way.

Suicide is not too strong a word to apply to the deliberate courting of death which characterises the tramp's career, because they are perfectly well aware that their lives must sooner or later be destroyed by the severity of the strain to which they are subjected. They share to the full the light-hearted willingness to pass out of this world which, as we have shown, is almost invariably felt by prisoners and the class generally from which they are recruited.

Such a state of feeling at first sight appears very unnatural and deplorable, but those who have had opportunities of gauging the unutterable sadness of most of their lives, can hardly regret that these poor people are able to look forward to death as their sure consoler and their truest friend. Their mental condition, and that, indeed, of most of the forlorn beings who drift into the Silent World, renders the problem of their possible permanent improvement, while within its limits, one of the deepest import; and we cannot but hope that the simple recital of their strange and sorrowful histories in these pages may have some influence in drawing attention to the subject.

CHAPTER V. A DREAM CRIME.

"The mountain tops in golden sunlight dying,
Whisper of rest;
The forest birds in silence now are lying
Each in his nest;
And motionless, by evening airs unshaken,
The forest crest;
Wait thou! and soon thou too shalt from life's heavy dream awaken
On the Great Father's breast."**THE** opportunities we have had from time to time of detailing our experience of the prison realms and their inhabitants, have not unnaturally drawn forth various expressions of opinion on the subject, which we are anxious to refute in so far as we hold them to be mistaken.

The first strong impression conveyed by the recital of scenes from a Silent World seems to have been—that work which implies continual associa– tion with the lowest and vilest of criminals must be to the last degree depressing and distasteful, and even to some extent demoralising. There is truth in this idea only as regards the pain which must always be felt in witnessing the sufferings and errors of our fellow–creatures, whatever may be their position in the social scale; but there is another aspect of the case which gives to labour among the tenants in our prisons an indescribable charm, such as could hardly be found in any other form of altruism that may be open to us.

The realism and energetic truth–seeking of this nineteenth century have, as we are all well aware, caused a widespread awakening to the inscrutable problems in the condition of humanity which surrounds us on every side. The complicated evils that beset our race are patent enough to all observers, but the difference of opinion among thoughtful persons as to the remedies which might be attempted for them, simply offers to us contrasts of a truly bewildering description. The most beneficent schemes are represented as doing more harm than good—while even the old–fash– ioned virtues of charity and almsgiving are denounced as mischievous to the recipients, and fatal to the good of the community. There is no doubt that this particular view is to a great extent borne out by recent experiences,—such as the disastrous results of the distribution, some time since, of the Lord Mayor's fund for the unemployed in London. The sixty thousand pounds generously contributed for the relief of starving families is said to have drawn to the capital hordes of the most vicious and worthless of those who live in idleness, abjuring honest work, and to have been for the most part absorbed by them, in spite of strenuous efforts to use the fund judiciously.

The discord of opinion to which we allude, however, obtains in respect to many burning questions: the higher education strongly advocated by some, is supposed by others to engender socialism and infidelity;—the rescue of the fallen is said to have the result of drawing numbers yet innocent into the ranks of the lost;—the strife of parties, the conflicts of Churches and sects, and many other opposing elements, combine to render the work of those who would serve their fellow–creatures in the outside world, a most discouraging and ungrateful task,—yet the enthusiasm of humanity has entered too strongly into the spirit of the age for these efforts to be abandoned, whatever may be the difficulties attendant upon their execution, and herein lies the charm of service done within the walls of a prison to the most utterly hopeless and depraved of human beings. There can be no question of their sore need of help and pity: they have reached the lowest depths of misery and degradation; they are without God, and without hope; they look upon all men as their enemies; they can fall no lower; they can endure nothing worse. Whatever, therefore, is done for their benefit, even mistakenly, must have a true value in contradistinction to their moral and physical destitution, which it probably could not have in more favourable circumstances. The faint gleam of light which would be wholly lost in the blaze of the noonday sun, is as a radiant messenger when it enters on impenetrable darkness. Prison visitors have the comfort of feeling that, as they alone have access to the criminals, what they attempt would be left entirely undone without their aid, and that their efforts, however feeble and unsatisfactory, must be better than nothing. Thus it is that tasks performed within the mournful jail, have a sweetness and attraction they could never have elsewhere. While the world without is ever steeped in mysterious evils, fettered and burdened by problems that may well make the most energetic philanthropist despair of accomplishing any good in his generation; it can, we think, be understood, that there is rest and consolation in spending an hour in the condemned cell with a man just about to suffer a terrible and ignominious death, so that he may feel—since even in that deepest abyss of misery he is not bereft of human sympathy—there may surely yet be hope for him, that mercy and pardon will not fail him at the feet of God.

If we can thus disprove the idea that prison work must necessarily be distasteful and depressing, we can still more strongly repudiate the theory which has been forcibly enunciated, that it engenders a sentimental "tenderness to crime." Some persons, it would seem, object even to any revelations being made from the Silent World on the ground that they are "gruesome," and that details of the lives of criminals can only be unpleasant and never profitable. Are we then to enjoy our brighter, happier lives, under the free airs and limitless light of the open heavens, and ignore the very existence of those who are lying bound in darkness and the shadow of death? Because they are a prey to the sin and iniquity which are the worst of misfortunes—because they are vile, their "souls cleaving to the dust,"—are we to make no effort to penetrate into the conditions of their hapless degraded existence, and seek such amelioration of it as can only be possible through an unreserved ventilation of the subject? Tenderness towards crime is the last feeling likely to be engendered in those who, within the walls of a prison, are brought into connection with it in all its unredeemed heinousness. But, in truth, the persons who make these objections are not really in a position to estimate the greater or less moral turpi– tude of the outcasts who are indiscriminately classed as criminals; their safe untrammelled lives can have no point of contact with those who, from infancy upward, have been in bondage to every possible evil influence. What, for instance, but an unreasoning, almost unconscious, abandonment to a career of crime, could possibly be expected for the offspring of one of our prisoners who had been sent to jail, in the course of a not very long life, some thirty or forty times? She had been steeped in sin from earliest girlhood, and the sole mode of escape from it with which she was acquainted, was the drastic remedy of suicide. She knew the name of God only as an oath; she had never said a prayer in the whole course of her life, and absolutely refused to be taught one, lest it should act as a kind of charm in compelling her to give up some of her iniquities. This woman had a child,—an intelligent little girl of four years old,—and she deliberately sold it for a small sum to a companion of like trade and position with herself, in order that it might be trained to gain money for its purchaser in the following manner: It was carefully taught to swear, and to lisp all the most horrible and disgraceful utterances it is possible to conceive, and then it was taken every night to one or other of the many public–houses with which the neighbourhood teemed, in order that it might be set upon a table and desired to amuse the men who sat drinking round it, by pouring out from its infant lips volleys of oaths and blasphemies. Was no tenderness to be shown to the criminality with which this unfortunate child was likely to be branded?—and the education of many of the inmates of our prisons has been of a similar nature. Another prisoner,—a poor forlorn outcast, who came into jail bruised and wounded from head to foot,—being strongly urged to give up some evil practices of which she was guilty, answered that it was impossible, **"because of the kicking."** Being asked what she meant by that expression, she explained that her husband was in the habit of kicking her so violently every day, that she was fain to propitiate him by any means, however unlawful, and to gain also, by stealing, the power of drowning the sense of her misery in drink.

Educated persons, writing from their well–ordered homes on criminals and the severity of punishment due to them, might alter their views and cease to be so much afraid of tenderness and pity, if they came into personal contact with such cases as these. They would find, indeed, that while it would naturally convey to them an almost appalling knowledge of the depths of infamy to which it is possible for human nature to fall, it would arouse in them at the same time a passionate desire to extend some species of aid to those of like flesh and blood with ourselves, who seem to have been forsaken of God and man from infancy, and could never, without a helping hand, struggle out of the mire in which they lie grovelling at our feet. By what means it may be possible to raise them from their degradation and misery is the one absorbing thought which must fill the mind of all prison visitors, to the exclusion either of disgust and depression, or of a sentimental sympathy with the perpetrators of crime. That is the problem they have to face, and it is one which extends in widening circles far beyond the prison walls; for it is evident that, if any moral or religious impression of substantial value is to be made on criminals, it must be of a nature to influence them through their whole future career, amid the temptations of the world on which they will ultimately be loosed once more.

In order to estimate the possibilities of this work, we have to grapple at once with a portentous obstacle, which can only be fully understood by those actually engaged in it: it is the difficulty of forming a right judgment as to the real nature and extent of the guilt which attaches to each individual prisoner. There is no more momentous lesson to be derived from a close intercourse with the criminal classes, than the discovery of the almost hopeless incapacity of human beings so to penetrate into the depths of their fellow–creatures' inner lives, and of the influences which have moulded them from infancy, as to be able to pronounce justly on their errors or innocence in the sight of the only infallible Judge of men. We may well doubt our power of judging one another, when, in the mystery of the complex human nature, it is perfectly possible for a man to live and die in absolute uncertainty as to whether he himself was, or was not, guilty of a deadly crime attributed to him. If this appears a questionable assertion, we can prove its undoubted truth by giving the history of a prisoner, whose singular case was made known to us in minute detail by the chief authority of the jail where he suffered for an offence of which he was from first to last entirely unconscious. It was, in our opinion, a **dream crime**—that is, a deed of violence committed under the false impression of a dream when the man was buried in profound slumber, not the smallest recollection of it remaining on his mind when he awoke. The facts are as follows:—

The man, whom we may call James Wheeler, had at one time been in good circumstances, but he and his wife both unfortunately became addicted to drinking, and their descent in the social scale was of course very rapid. He then became assist– ant to a butcher, in the intervals of other occupations, and at the time when the event occurred which brought the lives of both to an end, they were living in so humble a domicile that they had only one sleeping–room for the whole family, the children lying on the floor near the bed occupied by their parents.

One winter's evening Wheeler and his wife were both more or less intoxicated; but there had been no quarrel of any kind between them, when they went to bed with their children in the one room at seven o'clock. Wheeler immediately fell into a deep heavy slumber, from which, as his son afterwards distinctly stated, he never once awoke till three hours later. His wife meantime had chosen to take her supper in bed; and she carried there with her the knife which her husband used in his occupation as butcher, in order to cut pieces of bread from the small loaf which constituted her meal. While thus employing it, she put it down for a few minutes beside her, in such a position that it is supposed to have rested against the hand of the sleeping man. It is presumed that the touch of the instrument which he constantly used in the slaughter of animals, had engendered in his brain the dream that he was engaged in his usual duties. He grasped it unconsciously, and with one vague movement gave, what was afterwards emphatically described as "a butcher's stroke," to the living creature beside him, without awaking for a single moment from his drunken slumber. The eldest child, a boy of sixteen years of age, was aroused by hearing his mother moaning. He got up from the floor and leant over her. She was leaning back upon the knife, as if she had fallen against it, and was evidently dying. He drew it away from under her shoulder, where it was in fact embedded, without, however, it seems, apprehending that it was the cause of her serious condition. In another moment she had expired, still holding in her hand the last piece of bread she had cut from the loaf. The boy, greatly terrified, roughly awoke his father, who was lying unconscious in heavy sleep. Wheeler opened his eyes, bewildered and amazed, scarce able to take in the sense of his son's statement that the mother was dead. He sprang out of bed, and hurried round to the other side to look at her. When he saw that she had, in fact, ceased to breathe, he fell on his knees beside her, and burst into a passionate flood of tears. After a time his attention was drawn to the hemorrhage from her lips, and he exclaimed that she must have broken a blood–vessel. The cries of the children soon attracted neighbours to the room, and one of them, seeing the knife lying on the bed, asked Wheeler if he had stabbed his wife.

"My God, no!" he exclaimed; "I never did it!" All seemed then to acquiesce in the idea that the death had resulted from the natural rupture of a vessel; but next day, when preparations were made for the burial, it was found that a deep wound in the back was the undoubted cause of the fatal result.

Wheeler was at once arrested on a charge of wilful murder.

There was the strongest possible conviction of his innocence on the part of a very large number of persons; and this opinion was unanimously held by his fellow–workmen, who united in bearing testimony to the humane and gentle nature of the unhappy man. His children positively affirmed that there had been no struggle or quarrel between their parents, and that silence—broken only by the heavy breathing of the sleeping man—had reigned in the little bedroom from the time they all lay down till the sad discovery was made. That period, Wheeler solemnly declared, was to him a complete blank; he had not the faintest remembrance of anything that had occurred, excepting that he had gone to sleep at seven o'clock drunk, and awoke at ten, to find his wife dead.

The day of the trial came. He was defended by an able counsel, but apparently the prisoner, with the difficulty of expressing himself clearly which is common to persons of his class, had failed to explain that his absolute unconsciousness of the event pointed to the death stroke having been given under the influence of a dream, as the only solution of the mystery. A totally different theory was therefore set up for the defence, which simply suggested that the woman had fallen back upon the knife and been accidentally killed. Such an explanation of her death could not be sustained even by all the eloquence of a very clever barrister. Poor Wheeler's case was also seriously damaged by the ignorant folly of one of his neighbours, who, being bent on proving his innocence, persisted in maintaining that the woman had died, as was first supposed, from the rupture of a blood–vessel, after she knew perfectly well it was not the truth; for which benevolent lie she was adjudged five years penal servitude. We must be allowed to regret also that the unfortunate man did not fall into the hands of the careful noble—minded judge who tried Richard Hodson in a case we have previously described in these pages. The learned gentleman, who became the arbiter of Wheeler's destiny, took what he would have called a common—sense view of the affair. The woman died from a wound by a butcher's knife. There was no one in the room likely to have inflicted it except her husband: therefore he was guilty, and he must die. On these lines, the judge so vigorously charged the jury that they had no alternative but to bring in a verdict of guilty. They coupled it, however, with such an extremely strong recommendation to mercy, that they never for a moment doubted it would take effect in the reprieve of the prisoner. To their complete dismay, they found themselves mistaken; and the discovery that their verdict had condemned a man to execution, whom they believed to be virtually innocent, nearly drove one of their number out of his senses.

When the death—penalty was awarded to him, Wheeler stood forward in the dock, lifted his hands above his head, and said, "I am innocent!—ask the Lord—I am as innocent as a child. I am innocent—I am!—Lord, Lord! look down upon me—I am as innocent as a child just born."

Of course it is a very common occurrence that a prisoner vehemently proclaims his innocence on hearing himself condemned, and no notice is usually taken of such asseverations; but there was that in the tone and aspect of Wheeler as he uttered the words we have quoted, which carried conviction of their truth to the minds, we believe, of many who heard them, with the exception, it would seem, of the judge. He held to his preconceived opinion, and did so with unyielding determination till the tragedy was consummated.

The strange case aroused an extraordinary amount of public interest. The complete absence of any appearance of premeditation or of motive for the murder, rendered the theory that it had been committed under the influence of a dream the only reasonable explanation of the sad event. The popular excitement became so great, that the authorities felt it a duty to do their utmost to wring a confession from the man, if indeed he were guilty of the crime for which he was to suffer, and during the whole interval between his trial and execution, unceasing efforts were made to this end; but he never varied for a single instant from his deliberate statement, that he had not the faintest recollection of the period which had elapsed between the time that he fell asleep on first going to bed, and the moment when he was awakened by his son's exclamation that his mother was dead.

"I pray to the Lord day and night to bring back to my remembrance what took place from seven to ten that evening," he said again and again to the governor and chaplain of the jail; "but my memory is a complete blank." Wheeler was a religiously minded man, although he had given way to intemperance, and he did undoubtedly spend most of his time in prayer and in attending to the instructions of those who ministered to him. He was generally calm and resigned, but be broke down helplessly during his last interview with his children, when his youngest little girl produced her greatest treasure, a penny which had been bestowed upon her, and said she had brought it to "give to father," and she wished him to go out to the shops and buy whatever he liked with it. His brother went to see him a day or two before his execution, anxious like every one else that he should admit the crime; but Wheeler held out his hand to him saying, "It is as clear from it as it ever was—it had not a finger to do with it; it is hard to die like this." It was, however, in the very last moments of his life that he gave the strongest proof of his complete ignorance of the deed for which he was to suffer. The religious faith which he held sincerely was one of terror—he believed in an awful judgment to come and in a God who would infallibly cast an impenitent sinner into hell, and who was therefore more to be feared than those who could only kill the body. The morning of his execution had dawned—he was told that his hour was come. The hangman entered and pinioned him; then knowing what a widespread belief in his innocence existed outside the prison, and what a dangerous excitement it was causing, he made a last attempt to extort a confession from him, and said to him, "Have you anything to say? say these five words and nothing more!" The five words he meant him to speak were of course "I did commit the murder," but instead of uttering them Wheeler answered that he had said all he had to say to the chaplain, which simply was that the fatal evening had been from first to last completely blotted from his mind, and that he knew nothing whatever of the deed for which he was condemned. He was perfectly aware when he pronounced these words that he was in the very jaws of death—he could have nothing to gain or to lose in this world any more; and it is beyond credence that a man of his convictions could, for no possible reason, have been bold enough to plunge with a lie upon his lips into that dread eternity where he believed that an endless punishment awaited crime. The man only lived four minutes after making this last declaration,—and so departed. It is to be hoped that he woke from the painful dream of life to a brighter reality.

This singular history seems to us to illustrate forcibly the uncertainty which must always attend the attempts of workers in a prison, to estimate justly the guilt of its inmates with a view to their permanent reform; and the primary difficulty of forming a correct judgment of their moral and spiritual condition is enhanced by the fact that so many of them are systematic hypocrites, wonderfully skilful in rendering their countenances absolute masks to their real characters.

Nevertheless the work is not hopeless: even when it has to be carried on in connection with the most aggravated guilt, there are many cases which are singularly receptive of good influences.

It is necessary for the elucidation of the subject that we should distinguish between two distinct classes of delinquents, who come all alike under the heading of prisoners. There are, first, those who appear to be criminals of deepest dye—charged with murder, manslaughter, and other deeds of violence, or of living in continual villany and fraud; and secondly, those, for the most part simple country people, who are sent in under short sentences for very venial offences. Some of these latter cases are often most pitiable, and would rouse a strong feeling of exasperation against the "Justices' justice" which is so often denounced in the newspapers, were it not that the period of incarceration can generally be made morally beneficial to them.

We will deal first with the work which may be done among these comparatively harmless offenders, as it is undoubtedly the most pleasant and hopeful, and becomes often a lasting power for good to those it would benefit. It is generally found—even in the case of a first offence—that persons do not soil their hands with theft, or other malpractices, unless they have been living in much carelessness and indifference to the claims of religion and morals upon them. In their compulsory exile from all the interests and occupations of their home lives, they can often be led to consider seriously their position in the sight of God and man. They can be brought to feel that their first offence against the law has placed them on the threshold of a career of crime, from which it is but too likely that they may be drawn down step by step to graver deeds, till they sink in depths of evil hither undreamt of and unknown. If in that crisis of their lives they can be awakened to the claims of the great unerring Judge upon them, they are often induced to turn back of their own will from the fatal brink, and resolutely climb the steep ascent to the higher righteousness, whereby a lasting regeneration of their whole moral being is practically effected.

We can recall several instances where this was emphatically the case. One was a poor woman whose existence from her marriage in early girlhood had been a continual struggle to obtain the means of living for herself and her children, of which her husband's intemperate habits perpetually deprived them. Her life during all these years, though in no sense actively guilty, had been absolutely godless. She had acknowledged no higher law than the animal instinct of providing for her daily wants. She had never raised her eyes from the earth, to seek in heavenly regions for a better and a purer hope than it could ever afford her, and no true words of prayer passed her lips, either for herself or for those she loved. At length, on one occasion, when her husband had been longer than usual lost to her, in a low public–house where he spent every penny that should have provided food for his family, the woman was driven by actual starvation to her first offence against the law. She stole a small piece of meat from a shop, wherewith to feed her hungry children. She bad never been dishonest before; but from the moment when she committed this first theft, and passed the boundary–line between innocence and guilt, she became entirely reckless. She told the prison visitor afterwards, that had she not been checked at the very outset of a potential course of crime, she was prepared to fling all considerations of equity to the winds, and seek a living for her family by any nefarious means that might be within her reach. Fortunately for herself, the theft was at once discovered, and she was sent to prison for a sufficiently long period to allow of a strong religious impression being made on her mind.

The punishment was to a person of her loving sensitive temperament exceptionally severe, as she was parted not only from her elder children, but also from a young infant, whom it pierced her mother's heart to leave. Nevertheless, before she passed out from the prison walls, she was filled with the deepest gratitude for the blessings which her residence within them had brought to her.

She had known little of care or kindness in the outside world, and the knowledge which gradually dawned upon her of an unseen undying Love that was not only ever round her, but would have its fullest revelation in an eternal future, seemed to flood her whole being with a new and rapturous life. She hung on the words that were spoken to her on this subject with eager delight. She spent her whole time when her labour tasks were done in reading the Gospels, and in fervent supplications. Finally, as a result, no doubt, of her intense preoccupation with her new–found hopes, she had a vision one night as she lay asleep on her hard bed, which illuminated her whole being with a light that never more faded from it. She related this strange experience next day to her visitor, with a trembling awe and ecstasy that were too real to be mistaken. She had seen the Divine Redeemer, she said, clad in robes of dazzling whiteness—glorious in majesty, yet looking down on her with compassion and tenderness. She had heard Him speaking to her in words of consolation as to Jerusalem of old, telling her that her iniquity was pardoned, and her sins for ever washed away, and henceforth she was to follow Him in paths of righteousness, treading in His shining footsteps wheresoever they led her, through the dust and mire of this world's tortuous ways. That mystic command, however much it might have been the effect of pure imagination, she obeyed with indomitable perseverance. She went out from the prison a totally changed woman. We heard of her afterwards leading a most consistent and almost saintly life, striving to induce her husband to reform, and resolutely bringing up her children in the fear of God.

In the case of prisoners convicted like this poor woman of first offences, involving no great criminality, it is almost always possible not only to influence them for good but also to benefit them materially by placing them in a position to gain an honest living for themselves. We had a pleasant instance of this once in the case of two lads, sons of country labourers, who, in consequence of the agricultural depression, could no longer obtain even a scanty subsistence at home. In a fit of desperation they started one winter's day to walk to a far-distant town in search of work. After toiling on for many hours without food or shelter, sleeping, we believe, half frozen under a hedge all night, they rose to pursue their way next morning in spite of the weather, which, if we remember right, had culminated in a heavy snowstorm. They plodded on wearily through that day, while the gnawing hunger which had taken possession of them, alone prevented them from letting themselves fall down on some snow-heap and yield to the drowsiness that would have ended in the sleep of death. Darkness had closed in upon them, and they were almost in despair when they saw a light in the distance, and made for it eagerly, in the hope that it might be shining from a house where it would be possible for them to obtain a little food. It proved to proceed from a candle placed in the window of a farmhouse, to which they could approach very near in the snow without being overheard. They looked through the panes of glass into a room quite untenanted, and on a table close to them reposed a Christmas plum-pudding of most fascinating appearance and proportions. They had never been dishonest boys before, but this sight was too much for them. They found it quite easy to raise the window, gently seize the seductive pudding, and scud away through the snow without being seen. They were too ravenously hungry to go very far before they proceeded to devour their prize, which they did crouching down in the first sheltered spot they could find. There, however, vengeance was speedily upon them,—the empty dish, which had once contained the special Christmas dainty, was quickly perceived by the inmates of the farmhouse; the open window, and the footprints in the snow, led to the swift detection of the thieves; and before they had almost finished the delectable pudding, they found themselves on their way to the lock–up for the night.

As soon as possible they were brought before the nearest justice of the peace,—a country gentleman not, it is to be presumed, very learned in the law as it affects gradations in crime,—and by him they were summarily sent to prison for six months—a very severe sentence under the circumstances, but one that the two lads are now most thankful to have undergone. During the whole period of their detention they were systematically instructed in good principles, and at the close of it they were provided with an outfit and an introduction to an employer of labour in Canada, to which their passage was paid; and when we last heard of them they were doing extremely well, with excellent prospects before them.

Most of the simple people who come to prison under short sentences can generally be led, as we have said, to make use of their brief retirement from the world as a time of quiet reflection, which is very advantageous to them; but the form which their newly developed piety takes is sometimes rather embarrassing to their instructors.

A good homely woman, who was prospering as the keeper of a small shop in a country town, was sent to our jail once under circumstances, certainly, of considerable hardship. Her sole offence consisted in having received from her son some pieces of timber, which he had taken from the river where they were floating, and used them as fuel for her fire. They proved to be the property of a man who was utilising the stream as a means of transit for his wood, and poor Mrs Merry was indicted for receiving and appropriating stolen goods, her son having left the town.

The name we have given her best expresses her real designation, which had a most hilarious sound. Nothing could exceed her unreasoning horror and fear when she found herself actually within the prison walls. What secret tortures she expected to be inflicted on her cannot be guessed; but she seemed to look on all connected with the place as terrible agents of justice, whom it was necessary to propitiate by every possible means. When she was for the first time brought before the prison visitor according to custom, she suddenly, to the great dismay of that individual, dropped prone on her knees in the middle of the floor, and joined her hands in mute supplication to be spared the unknown agonies she expected to undergo. It was in vain that the visitor implored her to rise: she persisted in remaining in the attitude of a victim prepared for the sacrifice, and when an attempt was made to lift her bodily from the ground, it was found that the enormous weight of her portly person rendered the effort quite abortive. At length, however, by dint of strong insistence, she was induced to creep up from the ground and sit on the edge of a chair in presence of the formidable being with whom she had been left alone. After this concession it did not take long to win her simple confidence, and the flood-gates of her speech being unloosed, she poured out a complete history of all her delinquencies from infancy upwards. From that day Mrs Merry became the absolutely devoted slave of the person she had so much dreaded, and she devised every means she could think of to win favour in the eyes of her new friend. Some of her expedients were decidedly appalling. On one occasion she appeared with a beaming countenance, and triumphantly announced that she had learned by heart the whole of the first seven chapters of the Book of Genesis, and intended to recite them aloud then and there. Without leaving time for any remonstrance, she proceeded to declaim them in a high-pitched tone of voice with wonderfully glib utterance, and marginal readings of her own which slightly impaired the solemnity of the proceeding,—"Now the serpent was the most suitable of the beasts of the field," and so on. However, poor Mrs Merry did really, during the period of her incarceration, acquire a great deal of knowledge in religion and morals, which was likely to be of more use to her than the mere letter of the Pentateuch—the sense of which she never dreamt of investigating. Finally, she departed from the prison a much-sobered woman, and has led an exemplary life, we believe, ever since.

With these comparatively harmless prisoners the work is easy enough; but it is, of course, far otherwise in the case of men and women stained with the deepest guilt. Yet even with such criminals there are often remarkable instances of reform, which ought effectually to dispel any doubt as to the value of prison visitation, and the possibility of a permanent good work being accomplished amongst the more hardened prisoners. We will give two typical instances, the one of success and the other of failure, which are genuine illustrations of our position.

It has been truly said that when a woman is thoroughly bad and unscrupulous, she is radically worse than any man can succeed in being with his best endeavour; and we shall therefore select our cases from that which can scarce, in prison latitudes, be termed the gentler sex.

There came to the jail one day a middle-aged woman, well known to the officials, for those iron doors had closed upon her many a time before. She was considered to be an absolutely hopeless case—a coarse depraved woman, repulsive in appearance, blasphemous in language. She was brought to the visitor, as all the prisoners were in rotation, and as a matter of duty some words of counsel were spoken, without the least idea that they would make any impression upon her; but she seemed in a strange state of mental excitement, and suddenly plunged into a long account of her life since she had last been within those walls. It was plain, as she related it, that her thoughts were engrossed with one tragic inci– dent, which stood out dark and terrible from all minor events. The man—not her husband—with whom she had lived for many years, finished his dark career in a terrible manner, for he had hung himself in the one room where they had dwelt together, in the practice of all manner of evil deeds.

"Yes," she seemed ready to say, "he put an end to it all for himself: he had been a cruel man to me—he has knocked me down and trampled on me scores of times—but when I came and saw him hanging stone dead I forgot it all, and now—" The expression of her uncouth features seemed to indicate a terrible thought in her mind—"Now I suppose he is in hell—in hell!" She looked up, as if to put her dark doubt in the form of a question; but it was one to which no answer could be returned, only after a few minutes the visitor began to speak to her on that theme which rings for ever sweet and true within the prison walls. "The quality of mercy is not strained,"—mercy, to which all must be left who have passed to the secrets of eternity—mercy, still full of wondrous possibilities for her living self. Then she burst into a wild appeal for help to save her own sin–stained soul. She wanted to give up her past iniquities, to change her life, to do better, lest she should herself come to that place of torment—help!—she only wanted help that a way out of the mire and clay might be opened to her, an upward path to pure air and the sunshine of God's countenance.

The help was given, the way was made for her to leave the city, which had been the scene of all her guilt and misery, and to enter elsewhere on an honest and respectable calling. It must be owned, however, that this was done without almost any hope of a good result: the inveterate habit of intemperance, which had always held her in possession, seemed to prohibit the least chance of amendment.

About two years later, the visitor was called one day to see a very respectable–looking person who was anxious for an interview. It was a woman with a pleasant countenance, very well dressed in dark suitable clothing, who looked up with a smile, and yet almost with tears in her eyes, when she saw that she was not recognised. It was indeed the depraved criminal of the prison, who had never swerved from the path of rectitude on which she had entered when she left its doors. She was earning a good livelihood for herself by her industry and consistent conduct, and her superfluous earnings had enabled her to take a few days' holiday, in order to come and show her friend that she had been true to her word, and was trying to do right at last, with an honest and true heart—faithfully.

The second case, given in connection with that just recorded, seems almost to reproduce the story of the two women grinding in the mill, the one being taken and the other left.

A strong muscular–looking matron was committed to our jail for the manslaughter of her infant. There was no doubt that she had compassed the death of the child, for which iniquity she had justly received a heavy sentence; but it seemed to have been done rather through complete neglect and carelessness than from an actual mur– derous intention. She was, however, absolutely indifferent to the fatal result: unlike all other female prisoners we have known, she appeared to be entirely destitute of that pure instinct of mother's love, which usually burns as an unquenchable flame even in the most sin–darkened souls. Apparently she was rather relieved to know that by the disappearance of the poor infant she had a child the less to require attention from her; but in fact she had no room in her thoughts for the matter at all. The one absorbing topic of interest in her mind was her intense detestation of her sister–in–law, who had been the principal witness against her at her trial. According to her own account, these two ladies, mutually abhorring one another, had been in the habit of having periodical combats in the open streets of the town where they dwelt. The prisoner insisted on describing with the greatest gusto how they had been wont to challenge each other to a stand–up fight, and then retired for a few minutes to their homes to put on suitable garments for the fray, returning to the place where a ring was formed round them by an expectant throng: they would then have, as she expressed it, a certain "number of rounds," and would only cease when there seemed a risk of one or the other being incapacitated for renewing the fierce battle another day.

As may be supposed, the prisoner was summarily checked in these agreeable reminiscences, but there was no other subject which had the smallest interest for her. She evidently considered herself a champion fighter, and probably thought it fortunate that she possessed in her brother's wife a detested object on whom she could exercise her prowess. Metaphorically speaking, it was like trying to pierce the hide of a hippopotamus, to attempt to make any impression on the hard nature of this woman. She was compelled, as a matter of discipline, to listen respectfully to the admonitions addressed to her; but it was perfectly plain that she did not trouble herself to take in the sense of a single word. Her thoughts were far away, picturing, no doubt, the delights of another pugilistic encounter with her near relation, to take place as soon as possible after her release from prison,—and to that ineffable enjoyment she was in due time allowed to depart, when her period of detention expired. The conviction left on the minds of those who had tried to benefit her, was simply that in her they had one of the most striking instances of failure they had ever known in their experience.

Happily the failures are much more rare than the successes, and many pleasant instances of the latter might be given from the histories of a great variety of prisoners. The ceremonials of the Church which we are wont to associate with seasons of special rejoicing or solemnity were often called into requisition, shorn of all outward attractions. We will not sadden our pages with the annals of prison funerals, although they are often the means of strongly impressing the survivors, whether it be that ghastly burial within the precincts of the jail of men or women done to death by the law, or the gentler laying to rest of some forlorn criminal who has closed his eyes for ever on the dreary surroundings of the official sick ward. Scarcely less pathetic are the baptisms performed within the walls, of infants who will have to bear all their lives the stigma of having been born in a prison. Only one somewhat happier function is sometimes allowed us. In the case of young girls led into illegal practices by some unwedded lover, in conjunction with whom they were sent to jail, we had often the satisfaction of accomplishing a prison wedding, which placed them in a position to begin a new and better life with every inducement to a radical reform. The arrangements for these alliances had to be conducted somewhat after the fashion of princely individuals whose marriages are State affairs. As the bridegroom was incarcerated in the male side of the prison, and the bride on that reserved for the women, no intercourse of any sort was permitted to them. The negotiations between the high contracting parties had therefore to be diplomatically undertaken by grave official personages, passing from the one to the other, so that the wedding–day was fixed without a word having been exchanged on the subject by the two persons most concerned. When the day of their release came, which was also to be that of their union, they were met at the gate by the chaplain who was to perform the ceremony and the visitor who was to act as witness. The small procession then solemnly proceeded to the parish church, where the discharged convicts were duly united, and allowed to depart to a breakfast which, for the first time during many months, was not to consist of gruel.

We cannot close here without touching very briefly on a subject deserving of the fullest consideration, and which it is to be hoped may at no distant time occupy the attention of the Government, and be efficiently dealt with by adequate legislation. We refer to the condition of the children of prisoners, as the system which obtains with regard to them at present is eminently unsatisfactory. It is in truth one of masterly inactivity: the State simply ignores them altogether. Even when a man's life has been taken by the law for a crime which deprived his children of their mother also, these hapless orphans receive no official recognition of any kind. The workhouse is the only refuge to which they have a legal right; but they are not compelled to enter it, and the criminal associates of their unhappy parents generally take summary possession of them for begging or thieving purposes, and bring them up in all manner of vice. Private charity may at times step in; but it can only deal with individual cases here and there, and can in no sense cope with that vast contingent of the men and women of the future, who are left at the prison doors by their natural protectors, either to drift into the pauper's last home, or to be hidden in dens of infamy where a far worse fate awaits them.

It is scarcely possible for any one to traverse our country roads without being struck by the dismal appearance of the tramp children, who drag along their weary feet in the wake of their careless parents. The great majority of these poor waifs would benefit by any legislation that might deal with the offspring of convicts, as the race of tramps are at all times very prone to qualify themselves in various ways for a temporary residence within the prison walls.

This is a vast subject, of which the importance can only be indicated in the most cursory manner here; but we trust that the treatment of prisoners generally, especially with regard to their moral improvement and permanent reform, may soon seriously engage the attention of those in authority, and that some special provision may then also be made for the rescue of the unfortunate children of crime.

CHAPTER VI. THE DEATH PENALTY.

"If consciousness be aught, of all it seems to be,

Souls are something more than lights that gleam and flee."**ONE** of the most striking results of the scientific progress which has marked this present century has been a new revelation of the truth, that life and death alike are to us inscrutable mysteries, of which, it may be, the true meaning is as yet altogether hid from us. Side by side with this conviction, which impresses itself mainly on the cultured classes, there has been a remarkable awakening of the great mass of the people to all questions affecting their own rights and the administration of the justice meted out to them. In view of both these characteristics of our own time, it is perfectly certain that sooner or later the question of the continuance of the death penalty as the law of the land will be brought to the bar of public opinion, and forced with irresistible power on the consideration of those in authority.

The days have vanished into the past when the people of this country were submissively content to see the perpetrators of small offences driven in shoals to the gallows week by week, like sheep to the slaughter; and the time is now not far distant, when they will rise up and demand by what right judicial murders are to be committed in retaliation for those which have been the result of crime. To us who have been face to face with the death penalty, as it may be known and studied within the walls of the condemned cell, the question of its righteousness as between man and man can only be decided by a reference to those higher mysteries in the conditions of the human race of which we have spoken; but we will leave such considerations to the last, while we touch on the more practical bearings of the *lex talionis*, and the arguments by which it is generally upheld. The fact is admitted on all sides, that the advance of enlightenment and civilisation has surrounded the enforcement of capital punishment with rapidly increasing difficulties. The probability that in a short time we shall witness the establishment of a Court of Criminal Appeal, sufficiently proves that this is the case. It is felt to be a great anomaly that the mercy of the Crown should be lodged in the person of one State official, who has practically to try over again any doubtful case, while for those of clearer evidence he simply refers to the judge who presided at the trial, and who naturally reaffirms his former decision.

There is no doubt that this system is eminently unsatisfactory, and it seems to be extremely likely that the new court will be so also, in a still higher degree. Indeed, in the opinion of men of great legal experience, it will be found almost impossible to work it in accordance with the existing law as regards trial by jury. We may judge of the difficulties involved in its constitu– tion from the following words of the Master of the Rolls, who, in dealing with the subject, insists on five primary conditions. "The first condition, in my opinion," he writes, "is that the court should be the strongest which can be invented. To ensure this, it should, as to its members, not be a varying court, but should consist of judges nominated by the Crown once for all for life or until resignation. The number of the judges should be seven, with a quorum of five. The judges should be bound, in case of a conviction and sentence of death, at any inconvenience to other business, unless absolutely prevented, to attend in London within seven days after any such sentence, and in other cases at any time fixed by the president of the court. The second condition, in my opinion, is that the appeal should be as large as possible, on law, facts, and sentence, with the largest discretionary power as to any means by which, in the opinion of the court, it could be assisted to arrive at a right, just, and merciful conclusion. Thirdly, it should be declared in the Act that the decision in each case must be made to depend on the circumstances of the particular case. Fourthly, in my opinion, the consideration of mercy arising from particular circumstances—as, for instance, youth, extreme sickness, intolerable though not legal exasperation, despair—should not be excluded from the power of the court. Fifthly, the decision in any case should not necessarily be final, if after it new facts should arise or could be brought forward. Although I would allow the consideration of mercy to be given to the court, I would not take away the prerogative of mercy in the Crown to be exercised beyond and above the power of the court."

There is one obvious difficulty with regard to the proposed court which it requires no legal acumen to foresee. It is quite certain that when once it is known to exist, the right of appeal to it will be exercised on every occasion when a death sentence has been pronounced under any circumstances whatever. The remark of a woman who saw a notorious criminal being led to the scaffold, "Ah! but he was somebody's bairn," embodies a sentiment which holds good for all time. There is no living being, however brutal and depraved, who has fallen so completely out of the range of our common humanity, that there remains no one on earth who has an interest in his fate. How far soever he has made himself a curse, and outraged all natural affection, he will still to this extent be in touch with his fellow-creatures, that there will always be a mother or wife, a friend or brother, sometimes even a victim of his cruel propensities, who will seek to save him from that hanging by the neck till he is dead, against which there is so strong a sense of revolt among the lower orders.

It is clear that if there is to be an appeal and a new trial by a differently constituted body, in every case where the capital penalty has been awarded by the verdict of a jury and the sentence of a judge, the possibility of its retention as a legal punishment will become a very great problem. Nevertheless there can be no doubt that any proposal for its total abolition will meet with violent opposition from a very influential majority in the country. It is true that the extraordinary callousness and indifference to human life of former times no longer exists amongst us, as a rule. We have made a gradually progressive advance from the days, in Henry VIII.'s reign, when a thousand vagrants were hanged in one year for the crime of poverty; or from those of that eminently fatherly monarch George III. when, as an old chronicle expresses it, "a score or so of villains were turned off at Tyburn every Monday morning," and when Mary Jones, a young married woman with a new-born infant in her arms, was hanged for taking a small piece of cloth from the counter of a shop, which she restored on the instant when her attempt was detected. Even in the course of the present century before the change in the law, public feeling had not been much aroused on the subject. The writer can remember being told by a very benevolent old clergyman, that in his youth a man had been hanged for setting fire to one of his hay-ricks. Being asked whether he could not have obtained a reprieve for him as the prosecutor in the case, he answered quietly that he had not tried—it had never occurred to him to think of saving the poor culprit from a punishment in such general use.

In spite of the enthusiasm of humanity which is supposed to be rife among us now, we have not perhaps passed even yet very far beyond the spirit of these times—since a few months ago an astute politician, in conversation with the writer, strongly advocated capital punishment on the ground that it was the cheapest mode of disposing of criminals. It is to be hoped that there are not many who would share the views of this very economical gentleman; and we are quite prepared to admit that most of those who desire the retention of the death penalty are influenced by highly conscientious motives,—only we are satisfied that they are founded on absolute fallacies. That which undoubtedly weighs the most powerfully with all such persons is the conviction that capital punishment is a deterrent of crime. This idea is so deeply implanted in the sense of the community, that it seems almost in vain to hope that it may ever be rooted out. It is repeated from one to another by persons who have no possible means of knowing whether the assertion is true or not; it is re-echoed with parrot-like precision whenever the subject of the extreme penalty of the law is mooted anywhere. It sounds very plausible, and it is a truly comfortable theory on which conservative minds can rest their complacent acquiescence in the existing state of matters; but we desire to state in the strongest words we can use, that this argument in favour of the death penalty is absolutely and radically false. We do not make this assertion without warrant; our practical

94

experience has been very extensive. Even the few histories we have given in the preceding pages illustrate, so far as they go, the undoubted fact that crimes of violence are for the most part committed in the blind heat of passion by persons who are not in the habit of reasoning logically on any of their actions, and who never give a thought to the penal consequences of the deeds to which they are driven by the frenzy of the moment. Apart, however, from this practical obstacle to the deterring power of the legal murder, there remains the fact which we cannot assert too emphatically, that death is not the punishment which lawless men dread the most. Generally speaking, as some of the cases cited in our former chapters have shown, they do not dread it at all. Is there no significance in the truth that death is constantly being sought by suicide, and that frequently the means used to obtain the shelter of the grave is the very process by which the law inflicts its supreme punishment on the guilty?

In this age, especially when pessimism has invaded all classes, men not only do not dread death, but they often fiercely desire it. They seek it, they look forward to it as the cure of all mortal ills—the sure and painless refuge from the agony of life. Would that our legislators could be brought to realise the fact that, whatever may have been the case in former generations, the fear of death will deter neither man nor woman from crime in the present day.

There is, however, a punishment which is unspeakably dreaded by the class from which most of our criminals are recruited—and that is flogging. We believe that if the infliction of the lash, joined to penal servitude, which they also hold in horror, were to be the penalty for murder, it would have at least such a deterrent effect as any punishment can have which is pitted against the passions of men—and it certainly would operate far more effectually than the prospect of being relegated to the unconsciousness of the grave.

Independent of our fundamental principle that no dread of the capital penalty diminishes crime, the manner in which it is now inflicted is not calculated to make an impression of any kind on the people. It was undoubtedly a meritorious act of legislation when public executions were put an end to, with all the scandal of the disgraceful scenes which occurred on such occasions; but it is certain that any effect to be produced on the people by the fact that hanging is to avenge murder, could only be realised if the actual infliction of it were an open spectacle visible to the eyes of all. The private strangling or unintentional beheading of convicts in some disused cell of the prison or other hidden receptacle for the gallows, and in the presence of only half—a—dozen officials, is not a ceremony which has any impressiveness for the outside public, or, we may add, any appearance of justice. They are apt to term it in their phraseology a "hole–and–corner proceeding"—and so it literally is. While our legislators are calmly engaged with their breakfast on some fair morning, a handful of men, concealed behind impervious walls, solemnly conduct a fellow–creature a few steps from the bed where he has lain by night, and in some dark corner suspend him over a hole dug through the flooring, into which they let him drop with a violent shock and break his neck, or wrench his head off as occasionally happens. The waving of a black flag in the air for a short time as the outward token of this secret proceeding, is not a powerful means of arousing attention except in the most transitory manner. Thus it is that, unless some peculiarity in the case has created a special interest in the criminal, his death at the hands of the common hangman passes by with very little notice indeed, from those it is supposed to influence.

The idea strongly supported by some writers, that through the infliction of death for the crime of murder the public mind is to be educated into a sense of the enormity of the act, is an absolutely baseless theory which has no standpoint in reality. Even if such a result were possible in the old times, when a legislation of terror was supposed to be the only means of controlling the brutish masses of untaught, unreasoning people, it is a manifest truism that we have now to deal with totally different forces, in the intelligence and mental independence of our existing populations. They are much more concerned to criticise the acts of the legislature than to be morally influenced by them. In the course of the last few years, before it was decreed that executions should no longer be public, it happened that several of these ghastly tragedies followed each other quickly; and it is, we believe, a known fact that several of the men who then expiated their guilt on the scaffold had been present as spectators at the execution preceding their own, and had closely watched all the appalling details. Their own violent actions, in the course of a very short time afterwards, sufficiently proved that their education in tender– ness or morality had not been advanced by the painful sight. And here we arrive at a point of the highest importance in the question we are discussing; for we feel bound to affirm on the most substantial grounds that so far from the death penalty being a deterrent to murder, it operates, in fact, as an actual encouragement to it. It has the effect of destroying the intuitive sense of the sanctity of human life among the people. They no longer, as of old, look upon their legislators as infallible, and are in the habit of subjecting their enactments to a certain rough logic which cannot easily be gainsaid. They are disposed to take rather an ironical view of the singular arrangement which punishes the crime of murder by the perpetration of another murder in cold blood under the ægis of the law. Our working men, who now think and reason for themselves, are wont to say that if it is lawful and right in the authorities to kill a man deliberately because he has taken the life of another, it must be equally justifiable on their part to knock on the head any scoundrel who has done them or theirs some deadly injury, of perhaps a much more diabolical character. The fact that they do maintain this argument, and exemplify it by their actions, ought to weigh heavily in the scale against the continuance of the capital penalty. This element in the question was strongly felt by the late Mr Bright, whose hope was not realised that he might, as he expressed it, see the gallows-tree cut down before his death. Speaking on the subject, he said "that whenever the shocking punishment of hanging was inflicted, we weakened by so much that security to society resulting from the reverence with which human life is regarded."

Many of those who uphold the *lex talionis* do so on the high ground that it is a Divine command. A dignitary of the Church, who was most vehemently in favour of it, admitted to the writer lately, that unless it were the distinct ordinance of God we had no right to take, even judicially, the life of a fellow-creature. He seemed to have no doubt whatever that it was a decree of the Eternal Justice; but where, we may ask, is there any real warrant for such a belief? In these critical days, when every line of the sacred text is submitted to a searching examination, it is surely no longer possible to found this sanguinary law on one obscure verse in the earlier portion of the Pentateuch, of which the translation is so doubtful that it is quite open to question whether it does not imply a prophecy instead of a command. In those rude times, when the avenger of blood followed swiftly on the track of slaughter, it might well be predicted that whosoever shed man's blood, by man would his blood be shed. Is it not a very significant fact, in opposition to the construction generally put on that verse, that according to the same Record, the first murderer, Cain, was divinely sentenced to life and not to death? Supposing even, however, that it did suggest a command at that period, are we in our widely different days to hold ourselves bound by a single isolated enactment of a primeval Theocracy whose elaborate rules on other subjects we systematically ignore? It is simply part of the old Hebrew law, "an eye for an eye and a tooth for a tooth," which the Divine Founder of Christianity distinctly repudiated.

Another theory of the supporters of capital punishment is undoubtedly entitled to respect, inasmuch as it does breathe a certain spirit of charity, though arising from a merely imaginary hypothesis. This is the favourite idea that a man who suffers death on the scaffold escapes a future retribution, receiving his punishment in this life and passing to the Divine Judgment with an assurance, or at least a reasonable hope, of pardon which he could not otherwise possess. If we had any reliable ground for this belief, it might certainly go far to reconcile us to a law which cannot in other respects be defended; but the theory is a pure assumption, for which not a shadow of proof can be brought forward. Taking a common–sense view of the matter, it amounts to an attempt on our part to arrange the affairs of Providence according to our own ideas—and that is a proceeding which can hardly be justified even by the highest benevolence. Were it possible, however, for the advocates of this vision– ary argument to prove that it rested on a substantial basis, we should still hold that the powerful reasons which preponderate against the death penalty, outweigh a thousandfold everything which can be suggested in its favour.

We are at present looking at the subject merely in its practical bearing on the interests of the community, leaving aside the higher principles on which the most unanswerable objections to the law are founded; and dealing only with this lower ground, it is at once evident that the strongest argument against the *lex talionis* rests on the fallibility of human judgment. It is a fact which cannot be disputed, that innocent persons have repeatedly suffered an unjust death on the scaffold. In an article which lately appeared in the 'Fortnightly Review,' entitled "The Case against Capital Punishment," we find the following statistics: "Sir James Mackintosh, a most cool and dispassionate observer, declared that, taking a long period of time, one innocent man was hanged in every three years"; while the late Chief–Baron Kelly stated as the result of his experience, that in a period of thirty–eight years no less than twenty–two innocent persons had been sentenced to death, of whom seven were actually executed; and other cases are instanced where condemned men were only saved by the confession of the actual culprit.

It is not, however, only in cruel mistakes of this nature that the imperfection of human judgment operates most forcibly: there are gradations in the guilt which consists in taking the life of a fellow–creature, and there ought to be gradations in the punishment assigned to it. But no distinction is made between the heinous wickedness of a murder elaborately planned and deliberately carried out, and that which has resulted from a sudden stroke given in a moment of wild exasperation by a man driven almost mad through unendurable provocation. If the act comes technically under the head of murder and not of manslaughter, the penalty is the same. Recent scientific researches into the law of heredity have gone far to prove that propensities to crime may be the result of physical causes, even where they cannot be classed with cases of actual insanity; and how is any fallible human judge to discriminate as to the greater or less guilt of individuals so constituted? A punishment not irrevocable would leave time for the development of the truth. Apart from these more subtle difficulties, the inequalities of the justice meted out to our fellow–mortals under the law we are considering, may be seen and estimated in cases that are continually recurring. We will instance two that might be cited, out of numbers within our own knowledge.

Some years ago an elderly gentleman holding an office which entitled him to special respect was proved to have been guilty of the murder of his wife, under circumstances of especial barbarity. He had deliberately planned it for a long time previously: he had prepared a box in which he was to place her dismembered body, when he had with his own hands reduced it to the dimensions necessary for its concealment in that receptacle. During the days that he was making these cold–blooded arrangements, he was living in his usual daily inter– course with the doomed woman, sharing his meals with her, and passing his evenings quietly by her side. When the moment fixed in his long premeditation arrived, he fell upon her and slew her, afterwards disposing of her remains in the manner we have indicated. All these facts were conclusively proved, but the murderer was acquitted on the ground of insanity—a plea which later was known to have been much more than doubtful. About the same time a fine young man of excellent character, residing in a country village near the home of the writer, was brought to trial on the capital charge. He had attached himself with all the strength of a first love to a girl he hoped to marry. They were engaged, when a rival came on the scene, and the young woman, giddy and careless, with strong tendencies to the coarse coquetry of her class, openly manifested her preference for the new–comer. Day after day she found means to rouse the jealousy of her true lover to an almost ungovernable pitch. Still he had been forbearing and gentle with her through it all, till one evening when he was seated by the kitchen–fire in the house where they generally met, she came in, and after displaying her fondness for her new admirer, hurled every taunting and scornful epithet she could think of at her betrothed. Stung almost to madness, in one moment of fierce exasperation he snatched up the poker lying close to him and dealt her a single blow with it on the back of the head. It did not kill her, nor was it in the first instance in any sense a mortal wound, but he was taken into custody for the assault, full of grief and remorse for his momentary violence. The girl lived for a month, during the whole of which period her complete recovery was perfectly possible; but at last inflammation of the brain set in, and she died. The young man, who had not probably retained a spark of animosity against her after his one passionate blow had been given, was duly executed; while the wife–murderer, in full possession of his senses it is believed, enjoyed a country retirement at Broadwood, surrounded by every comfort.

We have very recently seen a death sentence commuted to penal servitude in a case which caused great popular excitement—mainly, it would seem, because the criminal was a person of culture and good looks. In grim contrast to her escape, only a few months previously a poor woman was hanged for a crime infinitely less heinous than that of which the lady was accused. Moreover, it became known at the time of her execution that she had been instigated to the act for which she suffered by a person who had unbounded influence over her, and who had indeed assisted her in the crime, though keeping himself well out of the way while the inquiry was going on. Yet not a hope of reprieve ever came to the unhappy pauper, born and bred in an obscure slum, where no light of knowledge touching anything in heaven or earth ever gleamed on her darkened soul, and where the struggle to get bread for herself and the little starvelings who had crossed her path without being allied to her, bounded the range of her ideas from day to day.

It will doubtless be affirmed that these inequalities in the administration of justice are quite unavoidable. It may be so; but in view of the fallibility and circumscribed potentialities of the human nature, have we any right ever to inflict a punishment which is irrevocable? Is it not enough that we are ourselves but blind creatures of a day, groping amid bewildering mysteries on the brink of that impenetrable gulf of death which awaits us one and all; and shall we precipitate others of our race into its unknown depths, because of the evil deeds they have done in that portion of their existence which alone is visible? Within the limits of this tangible life their crime was committed,—within these limits let it be expiated. And here we touch the grand fundamental reason which seems to prohibit human beings absolutely from the judicial destruction of life that goes by the name of the capital penalty. When we look this matter in the face, stripped of all its legal claims and the associations with which custom and prejudice have surrounded it, we see that in dealing death to a fellow–mortal we are inflicting a punishment of which we know neither the meaning, nor the issue, nor the extent. The pains and penalties which a man may be made to suffer during his tenure of earthly existence, can be meted out to him in precise proportion to the crimes committed within the same limits. We know exactly what we are doing in the retribution with which we visit his sins on earth. The whole transaction in all its bearings is open before us, and can be weighed and measured according to the most rigid lines of justice; but we are in absolute ignorance of the very nature as well as the ultimate results of the punishment of death, and there can, therefore, be no moral justification for its infliction by human beings on their fellow–creatures. Of the mystery of life we know nothing, save that we have not the power to create it or to bestow it on others, and consequently can have no right to destroy it; and of death we only know that it is irrevocable as well as impenetrable—that the day fixed by men for its consummation on one of their race is not that which would have brought his existence to a natural termination. He would have lived for an indefinite period longer, with what results to his immortal being in this world or the next we cannot guess. At our bidding, subject to the convenience of the hangman, he goes—where we know not, under conditions wholly hidden from us. Not knowing in the faintest degree what we are doing with him, we fling him out of our sight—out of our knowledge; we dismiss him from our responsibilities,—and with blind eyes and hands unguided, we hurl him into the mysteries of an inscrutable eternity.

It will be said that in what we have written against the existing law of capital punishment, we have been actuated by a sentimental tenderness towards crime—a weak desire to spare the murderer the tortures he has inflicted on his victim. It is not so. All who have the welfare of the community at heart, must strongly desire that evil–doers should receive the just reward of their deeds with all due severity. We have already specified certain punishments which criminals dread infinitely more than death, and that are in truth terrible in a far higher degree. Let their crimes be visited by these, and the sternest legislators may rest assured that justice will be fully satisfied; but let not a human touch, even by the impersonal hand of the law, be laid on the sacred, mysterious life which God alone can give, and God alone may righteously take away.

THE END.

CPSIA information can be obtained
at www.ICGtesting.com
Printed in the USA
BVHW02s1727181217
503123BV00007B/77/P